TASTING THE WINE COUNTRY

SHARON O'CONNOR'S MENUS AND MUSIC

TASTING THE

WINE COUNTRY

by

SHARON O'CONNOR

Recipes from Romantic Inns and Resorts of North America
Music by the Mike Marshall Quintet

MENUS AND MUSIC PRODUCTIONS, INC.

EMERYVILLE, CALIFORNIA

Printed in Korea

Library of Congress Catalog Card Number: 2001117468
O'Connor, Sharon
Menus and Music Volume XVI
Wine Country Dining
    Recipes from Romantic Inns and Resorts of North America
    Music by the Mike Marshall Quintet

Includes Index
1. Cookery 2. Entertaining
I. Title

ISBN 1-883914-33-7 (paperback with music compact disc)

Menus and Music Productions, Inc.
1462 66th Street
Emeryville, CA 94608
(510) 658-9100
www.menusandmusic.com

Design: Jennifer Barry Design, Sausalito, CA
Food photographer: Paul Moore
Food stylist: Amy Nathan
Prop stylist: Sara Slavin

10 9 8 7 6 5 4 3 2 1

Contents

🍇 FOREWORD 🍇

*C*an you really taste the wine country? You surely can. The experience will be a highly individualized one. It will involve more than the wine you choose and the food that accompanies it. Consider the following anecdotes.

The April night had become early morning. We gazed out the window of my apartment at the Manhattan skyline and agreed that it had been a culinary *tour de force*. My friend Arthur, arch-enemy of pretense, said as he shook my hand, "You were right to insist on black tie." The centerpiece of the evening's wine service had been a 1945 Chateau Gruaud-Larose in double magnums. We had opened the evening sipping 1976 Dom Perignon from crystal once found in the Romanov Court. The meal had been prepared by friends who own and operate a world-class restaurant in Maine. Did the dress matter? It did. It was a black tie evening!

In a recent conversation with Paul Lukacs, author of *American Vintage,* I somewhat sheepishly recalled my early days in radio spent in Western New York State quaffing copious amounts of the local wine. I remember celebrating Rosh Hashanah with my friend Steve and his parents Willie and Myrna at their home in Baltimore. We feasted on glorious chicken soup and roast beef and drank glass after glass of Great Western Winery's Catawba Pink. I was years away from Dom, double magnums, and Russian Imperial crystal. Those were salad days for sure and I remember them with great fondness and nostalgia.

Was the flagrantly decadent black tie evening in New York City better than the celebratory dinner in Baltimore? No, these two seemingly disparate scenes are united by a common element: mood. That's what Sharon O'Connor's marvelous series, Menus and Music, has always been about but here in the pairing of food and wine it reaches its zenith. Food and wine are laid against the backdrop of music, all three carefully chosen to achieve balance, even synergy, but the ensemble is incomplete. There is no mood yet. The process needs you. In black tie or denim; at an elegantly laid table or on a picnic blanket; in the company of fried chicken or foie gras; with an insouciant vintage or a lusty table wine, come create a mood and hence a memory!

Ponder this question: Is it possible for an inexpensive straw-clad bottle of Chianti to taste better than a patiently aged super Tuscan. Frankly not usually, but what if the Chianti were consumed with a pizza by candlelight in the company of your first serious love and super Tuscan was poured at the elegant and expensive dinner at which your spouse announced the commencement of divorce proceedings? The harsher Chianti would forever sing in your taste memory as surely as the super Tuscan would be eternally bitter.

Sure the world of wine is awash in rules and traditions. They arise from centuries of human experience and make good guides. They are however not the final word. You shall have that. I am often asked how one can learn more about wine. Are there credible courses to take? Should one attend seminars or find a mentor? You can do all of these things of course, but the very simplest way to learn more about wine is to start drinking it.

Put on the music, set out the glassware, lay on the repast and in the words of the old Russian greeting, "Please to the table!" assemble your guests. Now, pull the cork! As the wine gurgles from bottle to glass, you may hear faintly down through the centuries the question posed by Omar Khayyam the astronomer-poet of Persia:

> *I wonder often what the vintners buy*
> *one half so precious as the stuff they sell.*

The vintners sell memories and yours await!

—Gene Burns, Host of Dining Around, KGO Radio, San Francisco

INTRODUCTION

*D*uring the past year, it has been my great joy to explore fourteen North American wine regions and to bring chefs, winemakers, musicians, and artists together for this project! The talented and passionate people who are drawn to winemaking, cooking, music, and art make these grape growing areas into communities that celebrate life with concerts, music and theater festivals, art exhibits, poetry readings, and food and wine programs. And in addition to being great viticultural areas, each of these regions is a fantastic agricultural area where the ingredients necessary for excellent cooking are grown.

I asked chefs from twenty-one extraordinary wine country inns and resorts across the United States and Canada to choose recipes with the home cook in mind. I enjoyed cooking their delicious recipes in my own home and know that all of them can be made by a good home cook. Some of my favorites are Chilled Pear and Fennel Soup; Sauteed Scallops with Cauliflower, Capers, and Toasted Almonds; Salmon with Apple Mango Salsa; Spiced Rack of Lamb with Curried Sweet Potatoes and Spicy Curry Sauce; and Crème Fraîche Panna Cotta. I also asked chefs, sommeliers, and wine directors to offer suggestions for wines to accompany the meals. With or without these wines, I hope you enjoy making and eating these delicious dishes!

All of the inns and resorts in this book combine comfortably elegant lodging with an outstanding dining room or restaurant just a stroll away. Some inns serve breakfast only, but for dinner they are near one or more excellent restaurants.

These wine country hideaways are perfect for an escape from the hasty world of the city: they are places to forget worry, to read, to enjoy music and art, to be in love; they are places where life is celebrated! I know you will enjoy visiting any of them.

This is an exciting time in the history of North American winemaking. During the past few decades, there has been a revolution in wine technology and today wine science is almost universal. Skillful and devoted winemakers are making good wine as a rule, and great wine is coming from vineyards that don't have centuries of grape growing history behind them. Wine that is made to drink on a daily basis has never been better, and it has never been a better value for the money. Along with this increase in quality wine production, there has been a fundamental change in attitude about wine and in North American drinking habits. In the past, wine has suffered from an elitist image, while on the other hand, it has been associated with poverty and seen as a cheap substitute for hard liquor. Today wine drinking is synonymous with relaxation, leisurely meals shared with family and friends, and a healthy and graceful lifestyle. Although wine is a symbol of civilized living, it is not made for snobs and shouldn't be intimidating. Don't take wine too seriously— it's meant to be enjoyed!

The musical program recorded for this project captures the wine country spirit and makes it possible for you to bring some of that spirit into your own home. The performances are exceptional by any standard, and the music expresses a tremendous range of feelings, including anticipation, playfulness, contemplation, and absolute joy.

Combining three of life's great pleasures, food, wine, and music, nourishes both body and soul. Sitting down at the table with family and friends can offer the balance we need in a hectic world and unlock the key to relaxation. Wine, food, and music are also intense memory keys, and according to Nobel prize-winning biochemist Dr. Eric Kandel, "we are who we are because of what we learn and what we remember." In order to experience some magical, memorable days in the wine country, plan some visits and enjoy the pleasures of these celebrated regions for yourself. In the meantime, I hope this volume inspires many evenings of great music, delicious food, fine wine, and joy in your home. To your health and happiness!

—Sharon O'Connor

WINE NOTES

A Brief History of Wine Making in North America

Some of the first vineyards in North America were planted by Spanish missionaries who brought wagonloads of vines to California in order to satisfy the need for sacramental wine. The Mission grapes they planted were originally from Europe, although their exact origin is unknown. French settlers in what is now Quebec also cultivated native grapes as early as the 1530s.

By the late seventeenth century, American colonists had added wine grapes to the agricultural products grown in the newly settled territories. Pennsylvania governor William Penn planted a vineyard in 1694, using the classic European grape *Vitis vinifera*. Unfortunately, vines from Europe were unable to stand up to new world diseases and pests, and Penn's experiment was a failure. Another early viticultural pioneer was Thomas Jefferson (see box next page).

After the California missions were secularized in the 1830s, their vines were used to propagate new vineyards, particularly in Southern California. One of the first commercial wineries in California was founded in the 1850s by Charles Kohler, a gifted violinist of German descent. At first, Kohler worked as a violinist to support his Los Angeles winery, Kohler & Frohling, but by the time of his death he was a successful vintner and well-known civic leader. Another famous pioneer in the field

---

Vitis Vinifera

Most wine in Europe and North America is made from a grape stock called *Vitis vinifera*. Important varietals, or kinds of *Vitis vinifera* grapes, include Cabernet Sauvignon, Merlot, Pinot Noir, Riesling, Sauvignon Blanc, and Chardonnay. Some wines are made solely from one varietal, while others are blends. Native North American grapes, which are not part of the *Vitis vinifera* family, are hardier than their European cousins. However, the wines produced from native grapes are not suitable for excellent wine making. Today, most vintners in Europe and North America graft *Vitis vinifera* varietals onto disease-resistant North American rootstock.

> *We could, in the United States, make as great a variety of wines as are made in Europe, not exactly of the same kinds, but doubtless as good.*
>
> —THOMAS JEFFERSON, JULY 15, 1808

Thomas Jefferson was one of the first Americans to attempt to cultivate wine in the United States. During his stay in France, the statesman visited vineyards in Burgundy and Bordeaux and learned to enjoy a fine vintage as much as any Frenchman. Jefferson came to believe that European wine was far superior to the beer, whiskey, and fortified wines, such as Madeira and port, that were preferred by most Americans of the time.

Although there are records of several plantings at Monticello, Jefferson was unsuccessful in cultivating classic European wine grapes. He had to resort to importing the wines that had become a "necessity of life" and "indispensable for [his] health."

Today, the vineyards at Monticello have been restored according to Jefferson's own notes and other eighteenth-century American sources. Several vintages of Monticello wine have been successfully produced. Even more important, Jefferson's dream of a thriving American wine industry is now a reality. Wines from North America are respected and enjoyed throughout the world.

was Agoston Haraszthy, who founded Buena Vista winery in 1857. Nearly one-third of California wineries were founded by Italian immigrants, who shared the belief that family, friends, delicious food, and good wine were at the center of the universe. By the late 1800s the wine industry in California was thriving.

Wine making took off in the Northwest in the early nineteenth century. In 1825, Dr. John McLoughlin of the local Hudson's Bay outpost successfully cultivated wine grapes at Fort Vancouver, Washington. By 1836, French-Canadian settlers living near Walla Walla, Washington, were also growing grapes and producing wine.

In 1919, Congress passed the Eighteenth Amendment to the Constitution, which outlawed the sale of alcohol in the United States. Canada had passed a Temperance Act three years earlier, but the Canadian government did not classify wine with other "intoxicating" beverages. Vineyards in Canada continued to produce wine, and there was a lively trade in bootleg wine between the two countries for many years.

In 1933, Prohibition was repealed, but by then most American wineries had gone out of business. In order to repeal Prohibition, the United States Congress agreed to allow each state to set up its own governmental agency to regulate the sale of alcohol within its borders. Because of this decentralization, labyrinthine rules regarding the sale of wine from state to state are still in place today.

In Canada, the thriving bootleg industry prompted provinces to set up agencies controlling the sale of liquor, and today regulations still differ from province to province. In 1989, vintners in Ontario founded the Vintner's Quality Alliance to regulate production, appellation, and quality standards for fine wines in Canada.

For the first few decades after Prohibition, North American wine makers concentrated on quantity rather than quality. Little attention was paid to the art of vinification. In 1933, Ernest and Julio Gallo set up a wine production facility in Modesto, California. At first, they concentrated on producing bulk red table wine and then developed production and marketing strategies that made Gallo the largest wine producer in the world. Most recently, Gallo has expanded into Sonoma County where it is producing award-winning premium wines.

In 1938, André Tchelistcheff, a Russian wine chemist with a background in enological science and viticulture arrived from France to work at Beaulieu Vineyards in Napa Valley. He was struck by the unsophisticated winegrowing and winemaking there and worked to control fermentations and upgrade the winery's equipment. Over the years, Tchelistcheff produced dozens of award-winning vintages at Beaulieu. After leaving Beaulieu in 1973, he became a respected consultant, serving many California wineries, and in Washington State he is considered a founding father of the modern wine industry there. In 1966, Robert Mondavi opened the Robert Mondavi Winery in Oakville, California with the goal of producing wines that could match the best in the world. Within a few years, the winery established itself as a leader in the production of premium wines in Napa.

By the early 1970s, there was a small tourist industry based on California wine and the wine country lifestyle. In 1976, to celebrate the United States Bicentennial, wine merchant Steven Spurrier held a blind tasting in Paris. French experts gave two California wines, a Stag's Leap Wine Cellars Napa Valley Cabernet Sauvignon and a Chateau Montelena Napa Valley Chardonnay, a higher rating than the best French wines produced at the time. The California wine industry was instantly on the map and internationally creditable.

In 1962, Dr. Konstantin Frank began to experiment in New York's Finger Lakes region with vines traditionally grown in Europe's cooler climates, such as Germany and northern France. Dr. Frank was the first vintner to successfully grow *Vitis vinifera* vines in the East. Since then, vintners in cooler North American regions, such as the Niagara Peninsula in Ontario, the Okanagan valley in British Columbia, and the Finger Lakes, have discovered which *Vitis vinifera* varietals are suited to their microclimates and which vinicultural techniques are most appropriate for each growing area.

The wine industry in other North American regions has grown exponentially in the last few decades. In Virginia, cradle of the American wine industry, many varieties of premium wine are produced today. Oregon wine makers are internationally acclaimed for their success with the Pinot Noir grape, and Washington is the second largest wine producer in the United States after California. In British Columbia, vintners in the scenic Okanagan Valley are successfully producing fine vintages of Chardonnay, Merlot, Pinot Blanc, and other varieties. Long Island, historically known as an agricultural region, is home to many superb wineries, and chefs in New York City and on Long Island are now able to serve their dishes with locally produced wines.

Today, vintners in Canada and throughout the United States are committed to discovering how to best take advantage of regional climate and soil. In addition, figures such as Robert Mondavi are promoting wine as part of a healthy and gracious lifestyle and encouraging people to make wine a part of their daily lives. For many North Americans, good food, good company, and a glass of fine wine come together to make celebrations and family dinners complete.

If you think back to the best wines you've ever tasted, the setting probably had something to do with the experience: a glass of Cabernet Sauvignon at a romantic dinner for two, a chilled Chardonnay with lunch on an outdoor terrace in Napa Valley, or the outstanding Zinfandel you served at your last dinner party. In other words, there are many factors that affect the taste of wine. These include atmosphere, temperature, cultural preferences, and the tastes and aromas of the food served alongside.

Pairing food and wine can be as interesting as experimenting with new ingredients and techniques in the kitchen. Once you start thinking about a few fundamental principles, the best way to learn is through experience.

THE BASICS

Human beings can differentiate between only five primary tastes: sweet, salty, bitter, sour, and *umami,* a newly discovered taste that is sometimes described as savory. Discovered in 1905 by a Tokyo researcher who wondered why adding seaweed to soup makes it taste better, *umami* is a quality of deliciousness or savoriness found in high amounts in shellfish, meat, ripe tomatoes, aged cheese, and ripe fruits.

Each of the five primary tastes has a different effect on wine. In general, salty and acidic foods make wine taste milder and sweeter, while sweet flavors and dishes that are high in *umami* make wine taste stronger. When you increase the sweetness in a dish, you may want to serve a wine with some residual sugar, or a fruity wine that gives the perception of sweetness.

With these simple guidelines in mind, you can actually change the way wine tastes by changing the flavors in your food. For example, to make a dry wine taste sweeter, try adding an extra pinch of salt or a splash of lemon juice to your main dish. Conversely, adding foods such as aged cheese, seafood, and mushrooms, which are all high in *umami,* will make your wine taste drier and more tannic.

If you create a dish that balances the five tastes, the wine you serve will be unaffected by the flavors in the dish. It is interesting to note that condiments in each food culture throughout the world address the primary tastes and are used to balance dishes; from fish sauce in Thailand and Worcestershire sauce in England, to chutney in India and ketchup in the United States. If a dish has balanced flavors, the wine you drink with it will stand separately. For instance if you are making pizza, try to balance the toppings. If you use equal amounts of sweet and *umami* tastes—fresh tomatoes, mushrooms, Parmesan cheese, shrimp, clams, or anchovies—with salty and acidic flavors—olives, ham, bacon, or marinated artichoke hearts—the pizza will not change the taste of the wine you are drinking.

Pairing Food and Wine

Another way of thinking about wine and food is in terms of balance. For instance, when the flavors of a dish are particularly intense, a lighter wine will probably be overwhelmed in comparison. Conversely, a strong, flavorful wine can overpower the flavors in a delicate sauce. Again, remember that wine and food pairing is subjective. For some, a balanced combination where neither wine nor food is prominent is ideal. Other palates may prefer a lighter wine with flavorful dishes, or vice versa.

Some experts suggest that you identify the dominant element in a dish and pair the wine with that. For instance, poached chicken served plain, with a barbecue sauce, or with a mushroom and Madeira sauce will pair best with three quite different wines. Another way to achieve a rapport between food and wine is to add some of the wine you will serve with the meal to the dish itself. Substitute wine for some of the called-for stock or broth at the beginning of the cooking so that the alcohol evaporates and the flavors have a chance to blend.

Texture, spice, and temperature are also important factors. For instance, a light, acidic wine such as Sauvignon Blanc balances a rich, creamy sauce, and a refreshing summer salad is delicious paired with a cool white wine. When serving spicy dishes, you will probably want to avoid wines that are high in alcohol. Since spiciness makes the mouth more sensitive to all flavors, a strongly tannic Cabernet Sauvignon will taste harsher when paired with your favorite salsa or curry.

Developing Your Own Taste

An excellent way to learn about food and wine pairing is to try different wines with the foods that you have come to like over the years. Make something simple like pan-fried salmon with lemon butter and enjoy it with two different wines, for instance a dry and an off-dry Riesling, and see how the wines play against the dish. Comparing sips from two different wines is a great way to make a back-to-back comparison. If you are having a dinner party, serve more than one wine and let your guests compare and contrast while enjoying some pleasant conversation over dinner. Try serving two wines from the same winery, wines from two consecutive years, or wines of one particular year from different wineries. When the wines are compared side by side they become more interesting, and it is a lot more fun with friends there to help you decide which food and wine pairings are most successful.

Wine should be fun and accessible, not pretentious or put on a lofty pedestal. Stay open-minded and experiment. If you live in a place where making and drinking wine is an integral part of the culture, enjoying wine will happen as a matter of course. Some people just stick to wines produced in their own region. Others may want to enlist the help of a proprietor from a local wine shop who can introduce new wines. Wine writers also provide us with knowledgeable evaluations. But we learn by tasting wine, not by reading about it. So drink good wines, and your understanding will develop. Finding wines that you enjoy is really about satisfying your own curiosity and realizing what satisfies you. And remember: Satisfactory food and wine pairing also includes personal considerations, such as choosing to serve a bottle from the year of a friend's wedding or the same bottle you drank the last time you were together.

Pairing food and wine is an ongoing exploration and one of life's great pleasures.

A Wine and Food Tasting Party

In order to learn more about wine and food and have fun at the same time, turn your next dinner party into a wine and food tasting. It's an easy way to enjoy the company of good friends while deepening your knowledge of wine.

They are many ways to choose wines for the evening. A vertical tasting involves several vintages, or harvest years, of the same wine from one vineyard. You could also try the same wine from three or four different vineyards or regions. Or, choose two bottles from each of two or three types of wines, such as a Sauvignon Blanc from Sonoma and one from Washington, a Gewürztraminer from New York and one from British Columbia, and so on. You can also simply ask each guest to bring a favorite bottle.

Set an easy, informal table. A white tablecloth makes a perfect background for looking at wine, but if you're worried about spills, you can provide each person with a piece of plain white typing paper. Lighting should be low enough to create a relaxed mood, without being so dim that it's hard to see subtle variations in depth and color. Avoid highly scented flowers or candles that might distract from the wines' aromas, and provide pens and paper so your guests can take notes if they wish. Finally, your favorite instrumental music playing in the background will set the tone for a fun, informative evening.

Provide each guest with a small plate on which you've arranged a few slices of lemon, a piece of sweet apple such as Red Delicious, and a chunk of aged cheese, such as Parmigiano-Reggiano or aged Cheddar. Place dishes of hot sauce and small bowls of honey (honey sticks are a practical alternative) on the table. You should also offer plain bread sticks or crackers, plenty of fresh water to cleanse the palate, and spit buckets.

To make sure no one is influenced by label or price, wrap the bottles with brown paper bags and number each bag. Serve wines in pairs, preferably of the same type. This way, you'll have a basis for comparison. Your guests will find it easier to remember which wine they tasted first if you give them glasses with different sizes or shapes. And don't worry about having the proper crystal: simple tumblers will work just fine. If you decide to serve both whites and reds, it's typical to begin with the lighter white wines, making sure they are well chilled. A few ounces of each wine is plenty for tasting. Once everyone is seated, and the first wines have been poured, the tasting can begin.

As the host, you can make sure that your guests enjoy a memorable evening by leading the tasting and keeping track of the order of wines. Although discussion is an important part of a wine tasting, you may find it necessary to bring everyone's attention back to the wines, especially after the first few sips have been enjoyed!

Imagine all the ways you take pleasure in a piece of luscious chocolate cake. From the moment the plate is laid in front of you, you notice the beautiful rich color, the enticing aromas—and then, of course, the incomparable chocolate taste. There are just as many aspects to enjoying a glass of wine. Before you begin to pair wine with food, take a few moments to gather as much information as you can about the wines in front of you.

Begin by using your eyes. Pay attention to color, intensity, and richness. Then, before you even take a sip, smell the wine. Most of what we think of as taste actually comes from aroma. What words would you use to describe how this wine smells? Traditionally, words describing fruits, flowers, woods, and spices are used to capture the many aromas of wine.

Finally, taste the wine. Notice how the wine first hits your mouth and how the

---

Wine Ratings

Traditional wine tastings are conducted "blind," which means that labels are covered, and any identifying features such as cork or bottle shape are disguised. This allows the tasters to concentrate on each wine without any preconceived ideas about specific regions or vineyards. Usually, a tasting is confined to a *flight,* or specific group of wines such as several vintages of Oregon Pinot Noirs or Rieslings from the Niagara Peninsula of Ontario. The wines are compared to one another and to the tasters' sense of what makes an ideal version of that vintage or varietal. Wine ratings based upon such tastings can be a helpful starting point for experimenting with an unfamiliar region or type of wine.

tastes change after you swallow. What is your first reaction? Do you like this wine? Why or why not? Notice if it tastes dry or sweet to you. Along with flavor, pay attention to the "body." Some wines seem light and watery, while others are thick and rich in your mouth, like the difference between water and milk.

Once you have a first impression of each wine, you can start investigating what happens when you add other tastes. Take a bite of lemon and then try the first wine again. You should notice a marked difference in flavor. Does the wine taste drier or sweeter after the lemon? You can notice if the second sip tastes better to you, but try to be specific about what you mean by "good" and "bad" or "better" and "worse." Clear your palate with a sip of water or a bite of cracker. Taste the second wine. Then take another bite of lemon and try the second wine again.

Continue experimenting with the other foods and wines, discussing your findings and taking notes if you like. The simple act of paying attention will allow you to notice subtle differences in taste and aroma.

Once you've uncovered the bottles and discussed each wine, it's time for dinner! Serve one of the menus from this book or several recipes from different inns to make a balanced meal and allow your guests to choose their favorite wine to enjoy with each dish. Try each course with two different wines. If you like, you can provide lemon slices, salt, and if suitable, a fruit chutney or other sweet condiment with your meal and see how they affect the wines. Based on what they've learned, each person can flavor each dish to bring out the best in the wine.

Before long, your discussions will move from the Sauvignon Blanc's citrus aromas to that evening in Sonoma when you first tasted a California Zinfandel and the good time you had. Remember, the only rule is to enjoy yourself. We drink wine because it tastes good, and because we delight in the good conversation and convivial spirit it inspires.

How to Read a North American Wine Label

Labels help predict how your first sip will taste before you even open a bottle of wine. American wineries must follow wine-label regulations set forth by the Bureau of Alcohol, Tobacco, and Firearms. In Canada, the Vintner's Quality Alliance, or VQA, regulates the labeling of wine.

Variety: Wines can be named for types of grapes, also known as varietals. They can also have descriptive or generic names, such as Hearty Burgundy, Ruby Vixen, or red table wine. In the United States, if a varietal such as Zinfandel, Pinot Noir, or Chardonnay is used on a label, 75 percent of the wine must have been made from that grape. Canada requires that 85 percent of the wine come from a listed varietal.

Appellation of Origin: The appellation, an official name describing a wine's geographic origin, is listed with the type of wine. In Europe, the appellation is the most important information on a label. European wine drinkers can predict what a wine will taste like based on the location of the vineyard. Most North Americans are more interested in wine varieties than wine regions. However, there are official appellations of origin in both the United States and Canada. If an American Viticultural Area, or AVA, is listed on a label, 85 percent of the grapes used to make the wine must come from that region. In Canada, 100 percent of the grapes used to make a wine must come from the region, or Designated Viticulture Area, listed on the label.

Brand Name: This is usually the name of the winery that produces the wine. Larger wineries may use several brand names. Sometimes stores, restaurants, or companies contract with a winery to create a "special label."

Vintage Date: A wine's vintage tells the year when the grapes were harvested. In the United States, if a winery chooses to print a vintage on its labels, 95 percent of the wine must come from grapes picked in the declared year. In Canada, 100 percent of the grapes must be from the listed vintage. One simple way of choosing a bottle is to learn which vintages are considered good for various types of wine.

Produced and Bottled By or Estate Bottled: "Produced and bottled by" tells which vineyard actually produced the wine (not necessarily where the grapes were grown). "Estate bottled" means that the producer owns or controls the vineyards where the grapes were grown and that the winery is physically located at the vineyards.

Michael Masicampo

Long Weekend
Anticipation of relaxation . . .

Tra Vigne
Morning walk through the vineyard . . .

Sound of Sunlight
Time set aside for the important things . . .

Children's Song No. 6
*Nostalgia for mesmerizing whimsy,
impish excellence . . .*

Solera
*Celebration of the energy,
warmth, and sweetness . . .*

Vintage Niagara
After the crush . . .

Odeon
*Wine country café on a drowsy afternoon
and the mandolin player is there,
the mandolin player is always there . . .*

Piacenza
Sips to make us eloquent, lyrical . . .

Carmel
A message in the bottle . . .

Golliwog's Cakewalk
The feeling of childhood . . .

Minor Swing
That joie de vivre that you do so well . . .

Opus 2
*Deep, dark, rich—a red wine that
smells of the past, talks to the soul . . .*

MUSIC NOTES

The music recorded for this volume is as varied as wines from the North American regions presented in this book. I asked my friend Mike Marshall, a brilliant musician, food and wine lover, and amateur wine maker, to create an album of music that would celebrate the current excitement about North American wines and wine country cooking. From a selection of his compositions and other tunes he had performed in the past, I chose music that reflected influences from the world's great wine-making regions, and Mike made new arrangements for quintet, quartet, trio, and duet. The recording sessions with Mike Marshall on guitar and mandolin, violinist Darol Anger, pianist Philip Aaberg, Paul McCandless on oboe, sax, and English horn, and bassist Todd Phillips were an experience I will remember always. Mike Marshall and friends have given us all an album of amazing music for times when food, wine, poetry, music, and friendship come together.

You are listening to breathtaking invention by musicians who have played together in various ensembles for the past two decades. Their music is full of lightning-fast runs and astonishing technique; pure kinetic delight; shifts in tempo; soaring, ringing melodies; articulate counterpoint; and miniature tone poems of delicate, elegant tenderness. In sum, it is an exhilarating sonic reflection of the wine country and the joy that the art of wine making gives humanity.

Here is music to enjoy while you are exploring the wine country, while you are in the kitchen cooking, and while you are at the table eating some of the delicious dishes in this cookbook.

Carmel, originally titled Egypt, by Mike Marshall; Children's Song No. 6, by Chick Corea; Golliwog's Cakewalk, by Claude Debussy; Long Weekend, originally titled Key Signator, by Darol Anger; Minor Swing, by Django Reinhardt; Odeon, by Ernesto Nazareth; Opus 2, originally titled Lisa's Lullaby, by Kaila Flexer; Piacenza, by Darol Anger/Mike Marshall; Solera, originally titled Ybor City, by Mike Marshall; Sound of Sunlight, originally titled Song for Kaila, by Mike Marshall; Tra Vigne, originally titled We Three, by Mike Marshall; Vintage Niagara, originally titled Dolphins, by Mike Marshall.

About the Musicians

MIKE MARSHALL: Mike Marshall's touring and recording career began in 1979 as a member of the original David Grisman Quintet. A master of the mandolin, guitar, and violin, he has the rare ability to swing gracefully between jazz, classical, bluegrass, and Latin styles. Marshall has performed and recorded with some of the top acoustic string instrumentalists in the world, including Stephane Grappelli, Mark O'Connor, Béla Fleck, Edgar Meyer, and Joshua Bell. In 1983, Mike Marshall and Darol Anger formed the Grammy-nominated group Montreux, which recorded for the Windham Hill label and toured worldwide, and in 1986 he founded the Modern Mandolin Quartet, which made its Carnegie Hall debut in 1995.

DAROL ANGER: Violinist, fiddler, producer, and educator, Darol Anger is at home in a number of musical genres, some of which he helped to invent. With the jazz-oriented Turtle Island String Quartet, Anger developed and popularized new techniques for playing contemporary music on string instruments. The groups Psychograss, New Grange, and the Anger-Marshall Band feature his compositions and arrangements. Anger was a member of the original David Grisman Band, which created a new genre of acoustic string band music. Anger holds the String Chair of the International Association of Jazz Educators.

PAUL MCCANDLESS: During a distinguished career spanning three decades, Paul McCandless's playing and composing has been integral to the ensemble sound of two seminal world music bands, the original Paul Winter Consort and the innovative quartet Oregon. A gifted multi-instrumentalist, McCandless's primary instruments are the oboe, English horn, and saxophone, and he can be heard on albums and performances with such musicians as Jaco Pastorius, Art Lande, Wynton Marsalis, Pat Metheny, Steve Reich, Al Jarreau, and String Cheese Incident. In 1996, he won a Grammy with Béla Fleck for Best Pop Instrumental, and as a Windham Hill recording artist, he contributed to numerous anthologies, two of which were gold records.

PHILIP AABERG: Since graduating from Harvard University with a Bachelor of Arts in music, pianist Philip Aaberg has performed piano concertos with the Boston Pops Orchestra and appeared with stars such as Peter Gabriel, Elvin Bishop, and

John Hiatt. As a recording artist, he has crossed traditional aesthetic boundaries and can be heard on everything from best-selling pop and country albums to contemporary chamber music and experimental jazz projects. Aaberg's performance on the PBS program, All-American Jazz, was nominated for an Emmy. A Montana native, he composed the soundtrack of "To Kill a Mockingbird" for the Montana Repertory Theater, and over a period of years he has worked closely with the Paul Dresher Ensemble.

Todd Phillips: Over the past twenty-three years, Todd Phillips has been the acoustic bassist of choice on both innovative and traditional acoustic bluegrass recordings. Phillips performed for five years with the original David Grisman Quintet, followed by five years with the Tony Rice Unit. He has worked with Vassar Clements, Ricky Skaggs, Stephane Grappelli, Sam Bush, and Kate Wolf, among others. He received a Grammy Award in 1983 for Country Instrumental of the Year with the group The New South, and a second Grammy in 1996 for producing the Bluegrass Album of the Year, *True Life Blues, The Songs of Bill Monroe.*

The Aerie Resort

Malahat, British Columbia

Nestled high in the mountains of Southern Vancouver Island and just thirty minutes from the capital city of Victoria, the Aerie has gained an international reputation for luxurious accommodations, extraordinary dining, a European-style spa, and unforgettable views of snow-capped mountains and Pacific fjords. The gorgeous setting inspired Austrian-born Maria Schuster to create a luxurious Mediterranean-style estate, and in 1990 she began the building of her dream. Today, the renowned Aerie Resort is managed by her son, Markus Griesser, and since 1995 it has been a member of the prestigious Relais & Chateaux Association.

The Aerie's guest rooms and suites offer the highest level of personal comfort and breathtaking views from private decks. Guests enjoy the resort's Aveda Wellness and Beauty Center, sauna, indoor pool, and ten acres of meticulously kept grounds. Vancouver Island and the nearby Gulf Islands offer many opportunities for exploration and relaxation, including sailing, scuba diving, kayaking, horseback riding, mountain biking, and golfing. Visitors also enjoy tours of local wineries and farms, eco-adventures, and native arts and heritage tours.

Executive chef Christophe Letard's brilliant cooking reflects the influence of traditional French techniques and fresh flavors of the Pacific Northwest. Served in the Aerie's elegant dining room, his innovative seasonal menus take full advantage of locally grown products, from seafood and game to fresh morels and berries. Wine director James Kendal has developed the restaurant's extensive wine list and will gladly pair wines with each course of chef Letard's menu. Focusing on local British Columbia and Pacific Northwest wines, as well as those from California and France, the list has received *Wine Spectator* magazine's Award of Excellence. Chef Letard and wine director Kendal host the Aerie's annual wine dinner, a five-course tasting menu and wine pairing that is a gastronomic extravaganza. The following recipes were created by chef Christophe Letard.

Menu

Chilled Pear and Fennel Soup with Gravlax

BURROWING OWL PINOT GRIS, 1998

❧

Veal Tenderloin Roast
with Salsify and Artichoke Pesto Crisps

CEDAR CREEK PINOT NOIR PLATINUM RESERVE, 1998

❧

Blackberry Jam and Chocolate Ganache Tart
with Marinated Berries

VENTURI-SCHULZE #3, 1999

Chilled Pear and Fennel Soup with Gravlax

A delicate, intriguing combination of flavors that creates a memorable soup. Gravlax is a traditional Scandinavian dish of salmon cured with herbs, salt, pepper, sugar, and citrus juice. If you don't have time to make the gravlax, smoked salmon may be substituted.

4 tablespoons (2 oz/60 g) unsalted butter
1 onion, chopped
2 celery stalks, chopped
3 leeks, white part only, sliced
1 fennel bulb, trimmed and thinly sliced crosswise
½ cup (4 fl oz/125 ml) dry white wine
3 cups water
3 pears, peeled and cored
2 star anise
2 green cardamom pods
1 cup (8 fl oz/250 ml) heavy cream
Salt and freshly ground pepper to taste
1 tablespoon minced fresh dill
Gravlax (recipe follows)

➤ In a large saucepan, melt the butter over medium-low heat, and add the onion, celery, leeks, and fennel. Cover and cook for 5 minutes, stirring frequently. Pour in the wine and cook for 5 minutes. Add the water and simmer for 20 minutes.

➤ Chop 2 of the pears and add to the soup. Tie the star anise and cardamom in a cheesecloth square. Add the cheesecloth sachet, cream, salt, and pepper to the soup and cook for 10 minutes. Remove the sachet. In batches, transfer the soup to a blender or food processor and purée. Strain the soup through a fine-mesh sieve, pressing on the solids with the back of a large spoon. Taste and adjust the seasoning. Let cool, cover, and refrigerate for 2 hours to chill.

➤ Finely dice the remaining pear. In a small bowl, combine the pear, chopped dill, and 1 tablespoon of the gravlax marinade.

➤ Ladle the soup into shallow bowls and place a salmon square in the center of each bowl. Sprinkle the pear mixture and minced dill over the soup.

Makes 4 servings

GRAVLAX

Begin marinating the salmon 12 to 24 hours before you plan to serve it.

One 8-ounce (250-g) salmon fillet, pin bones and skin removed
¼ cup (2 oz/60 g) sugar
3 tablespoons salt
3 tablespoons olive oil
3 tablespoons walnut oil
Juice of 1 lemon
Juice of 1 lime
3 black peppercorns
½ teaspoon coriander seeds, crushed
1 tablespoon *each* minced fresh dill, cilantro, and chives

Lay the salmon on a piece of plastic wrap. In a small bowl, stir the sugar, salt, oils, juices, peppercorns, and coriander seeds together. Rub the salmon on both sides with the mixture. Turn flesh side up and top with the dill, cilantro, and chives. Wrap the salmon in the plastic and place on a clean plate. Top with a second plate and place a 2-to 3-pound (1- to 1.5-kg) weight on top (canned food works well). Refrigerate until the fish is somewhat opaque, 12 to 24 hours. To serve, scrape off all the seasonings and pat dry. Thinly slice the salmon crosswise and cut into squares. *Makes 8 ounces (250 g)*

ANNE MILLER

Veal Tenderloin Roast
with Salsify and Artichoke Pesto Crisps

The crisps can be baked at the same time as the veal tenderloin is roasting.

One 1½-pound (750-g) veal tenderloin, trimmed of fat and silver skin
2 garlic cloves
1 bay leaf
1 tablespoon chopped fresh thyme
1 teaspoon salt
½ teaspoon freshly ground pepper
4 tablespoons olive oil

Pinot Noir Jus
4 tablespoons unsalted butter
4 shallots, minced
1 garlic clove, minced
¾ cup (3 oz/90 g) fresh elderberries or blueberries
1 thyme sprig, chopped
2 cups (16 fl oz/500 ml) dry red wine, preferably Pinot Noir
3 cups (24 fl oz/750 ml) veal stock (see Basics) or canned low-salt beef broth
Salt and freshly ground pepper to taste

Spinach
1 tablespoon unsalted butter
1 garlic clove, minced
1 large bunch spinach, stemmed

4 rosemary sprigs for garnish
Salsify and Artichoke Pesto Crisps (recipe follows)

Tie the tenderloin with kitchen string to form a cylinder. In a mortar, combine the garlic, bay leaf, thyme, salt, and pepper. Crush with a pestle. Stir in 3 tablespoons of the olive oil. Rub the mixture all over the veal, cover the meat with plastic wrap, and refrigerate for 2 to 6 hours. Remove from the refrigerator 30 minutes before roasting.

(continued on following page)

❧ Preheat the oven to 425°F (220°C). Heat a large ovenproof frying pan over medium-high heat for 2 minutes. Add the remaining 1 tablespoon olive oil and brown the veal tenderloin on all sides. Transfer the pan to the preheated oven and bake for 10 to 12 minutes, or until an instant-read thermometer registers 165°F (70°C). Transfer the roast to a plate and loosely cover with aluminum foil; let rest for 10 minutes.

❧ To make the jus: In a large frying pan, melt 3 tablespoons of the butter over medium-low heat and sauté the shallots, garlic, berries, and thyme for 3 minutes. Add the wine, raise heat to high, and boil until reduced to a glaze. Add the stock or broth and boil until reduced by half. Season with salt and pepper. Strain and set aside.

❧ To make the spinach: In a large nonreactive frying pan, melt the butter over medium-high heat and sauté the garlic for 1 minute, or until fragrant. Add the spinach and sauté until just wilted; remove from heat and cover to keep warm.

❧ To serve, swirl the remaining 1 tablespoon butter into the jus and melt over low heat. Cut the veal tenderloin into 12 slices. Place a crisp and a nest of spinach at the top of each of 4 warmed plates. Garnish the spinach with a rosemary sprig. Fan 3 slices of veal tenderloin over the lower part of each plate and spoon a line of jus between the meat and spinach; serve immediately.

Makes 4 servings

SALSIFY AND ARTICHOKE PESTO CRISPS

6 ounces (185 g) salsify,* peeled
Juice of 1 lemon
4 cooked artichoke hearts (see Basics)
1 shallot, minced
2 green onions, white part only, chopped
¼ cup (½ oz/15 g) minced fresh flat-leaf parsley
2 tablespoons black truffle oil
Salt and freshly ground pepper to taste
2 thawed frozen phyllo dough sheets
⅓ cup (3 oz/90 g) clarified butter, melted (see Basics)

Preheat the oven to 425°F (220°C). Drop the salsify into a pan of boiling water and add the lemon juice. Cook for 10 minutes, or until tender. Drain, let cool, and coarsely chop. In a blender or food processor, combine the salsify, artichoke hearts, shallot, green onion, parsley, truffle oil, and salt and pepper. Purée until smooth.

Cut the 2 phyllo sheets in half crosswise and brush lightly with clarified butter. Fold the sheets in half and mold the phyllo into two 2½-inch-diameter (6-cm) ring molds. Fill each with ½ cup (4 oz/125 g) of the pesto. Fold the phyllo over the filling. Transfer to a baking sheet, folded side down. Repeat to make 2 more crisps. Bake for 8 to 10 minutes, or until golden brown. Serve warm.

Makes 4 servings

*Salsify, also called oyster plant, is a root vegetable with a delicate oysterlike flavor. Look for it in specialty food markets.

Blackberry Jam and Chocolate Ganache Tart with Marinated Berries

At the Aerie, freshly made jam gives this summertime treat an extra dimension, but the tart is also delicious made with purchased blackberry jam.

Sweet Pastry Dough
1¾ cups (9 oz/280 g) all-purpose flour
⅔ cup (5 oz/155 g) cold unsalted butter
⅓ cup (3 oz/90 g) sugar
¼ teaspoon salt
1 egg

Blackberry Jam
1 cup (4 oz/125 g) fresh blackberries
½ cup (4 fl oz/125 ml) water
Juice of ½ lemon
1 cup (8 oz/250 g) sugar

Dark Chocolate Ganache
⅔ cup (5 fl oz/150 ml) heavy cream
10 ounces (315 g) bittersweet chocolate, chopped
½ cup (4 oz/125 g) cold unsalted butter, diced
2 tablespoons Grand Marnier

Marinated Berries
Grated zest and juice of 2 oranges
¼ cup (3 oz/90 g) honey
2 tablespoons Grand Marnier or other orange liqueur
½ cup (2 oz/60 g) fresh blackberries
½ cup (2 oz/60 g) fresh blueberries

Mint sprigs for garnish

To make the pastry: In a food processor, combine the flour, butter, sugar, and salt and process for 15 seconds, or until the mixture resembles coarse crumbs. With the machine running, add the egg and process just until the dough forms a ball, about 20 seconds. Flatten the dough into a disk, cover with plastic wrap or place in a self-sealing plastic bag, and refrigerate for at least 30 minutes or overnight.

To make the jam: In a heavy, medium saucepan, combine all the ingredients and cook over medium heat for about 15 minutes, stirring occasionally until thickened. Let cool.

On a lightly floured surface, roll the dough into an 11-inch (28-cm) circle. Fit into a 10-inch (23-cm) tart pan. Run the rolling pin over the top of the pan to trim the edges. Prick the pastry with a fork and refrigerate for 30 minutes. Preheat the oven to 350°F (180°C). Line the pastry shell with aluminum foil and fill with dried beans or pastry weights. Bake for 20 minutes, or until set and very lightly browned. Remove the beans or weights and foil. Prick the pastry with a fork again and bake for 10 minutes, or until golden brown. Let cool. Spoon the jam into the pastry shell.

To make the ganache: In a small, heavy saucepan, bring the cream to a boil over medium-low heat. Remove from heat and whisk in the chocolate and butter until smooth. Stir in the Grand Marnier. Pour the chocolate mixture into the pastry shell and refrigerate until set, about 1 hour.

To make the marinated berries: In a medium saucepan, bring the orange zest and juice, honey, and Grand Marnier to a boil. Remove from heat and stir in the berries. Let sit for 15 minutes. Using a slotted spoon, spoon the berries over the tart.

Cut the tart into wedges and garnish each serving with a mint sprig.

Makes one 10-inch (25-cm) tart

Who loves not woman, wine and song,
Remains a fool his whole life long.

—MARTIN LUTHER

Applewood Inn & Restaurant

Guerneville, California

Located along the Russian River Wine Road, Applewood is a relaxed hideaway where guests enjoy stylish accommodations, exceptional dining, and the pleasures of peace and quiet. Just an hour and a half north of San Francisco, the inn is surrounded by majestic redwood trees and is near more than seventy-five award-winning wineries. Designed by Jack Warnecke and built in 1922, the inn has been carefully restored and expanded since 1985 by Darryl Notter and Jim Caron, the engaging owners who personally manage the inn and oversee every detail.

Applewood's charming rooms and suites are housed in historic Belden House and two Mediterranean-style villas, Piccolo Casa and the Gate House, which surround a tranquil inner courtyard with a bubbling fountain. Guests enjoy swims in the pool and relaxing strolls through the six-acre property, with its large organic garden and fruit tree orchard. While visiting the hidden-away wineries of the Russian River appellation, visitors often happen on some tasting rooms while looking for others, but the meandering is as much fun as the tasting. Applewood is just minutes from the ancient redwood trees of Armstrong Woods, a seven-hundred-acre state park, and a short drive from the secluded beaches and spectacular sheer cliffs of the rugged Sonoma coast.

At the end of the day, guests assemble for a convivial tasting of selected wines before dinner in the restaurant. With its copper-topped wine bar, two river-rock fireplaces, lofty beamed ceilings, and gorgeous views of the redwoods, the restaurant is a wonderful setting for chef Brian Gerritsen's deeply-flavored seasonal cooking. Cocktails and early dinners can be enjoyed al fresco on the deck that overlooks the garden, and in the morning gourmet breakfasts are served in the dining room. Chef Gerritsen's menus are inspired by French, Italian, and Spanish wine country cuisine and based on the best available regional ingredients. Each afternoon he walks down to the inn's prolific garden to gather fruit, vegetables, and herbs for the evening meal. Applewood's wine list features Sonoma County varietals and is a primer in Russian River wines. Proprietor Jim Caron, an avid wine collector, happily gives tours of the downstairs wine cellar, which is a recipient of *Wine Spectator* magazine's Award of Excellence. Executive chef Brian Gerritsen created the following dinner menu for Menus and Music.

Kistler
Vine Hill Vineyard
Russian River Valley
No. 1997
22,488 bottles of this vintage were produced

MERRY EDWARDS
1998
RUSSIAN RIVER VALLEY
PINOT NOIR
ALCOHOL 13.9% BY VOLUME

TOPOLOS
Russian River Valley
Zinfandel
Piner Heights
1997
PRODUCED & BOTTLED BY TOPOLOS
AT RUSSIAN RIVER VINEYARDS, FORESTVILLE, CA, USA
ALCOHOL 15.0% BY VOLUME - CONTAINS SULFITES

KORBEL
Natural
Sonoma County Champagne
60% PINOT NOIR
40% CHARDONNAY
I
PRODUCED AND BOTTLED BY F. KORBEL & BROS. INC. GUERNEVILLE, SONOMA CO., CALIFORNIA • ALCOHOL 12 % BY VOL

1999
RUSSIAN
RIVER
VALLEY
PINOT NOIR
ESTATE BOTTLED
J

DE LOACH
1 9 9 9
ESTATE BOTTLED
CHARDONNAY
RUSSIAN RIVER VALLEY
OLIVET RANCH

HOP KILN
1998
RUSSIAN RIVER VALLEY
CABERNET SAUVIGNON
ESTATE GROWN~M. GRIFFIN VINEYARD
14.1% ALCOHOL BY VOLUME

MATANZAS CREEK WINERY
1998 Merlot
Sonoma Valley

HANNA
1999
Pinot Noir
RUSSIAN RIVER VALLEY
Estate Grown
ALCOHOL
BY
VOLUME
14.2%

1999
Russian River Valley
BELVEDERE
CHARDONNAY
There is no single recipe for making delicious wine, only the energy between land and grape, and our winemakers vision to bring it from vine to bottle.

DAVIS BYNUM
2000
RUSSIAN RIVER VALLEY
FUME BLANC
SHONE FARM
ALC. 13.0% BY VOL.

VINTAGE 1997
The Cutrer
APPELLATION RUSSIAN RIVER VALLEY
ESTATE BOTTLED
SONOMA - CUTRER
RUSSIAN RIVER VALLEY CHARDONNAY BOTTLED BY SONOMA-CUTRER, WINDSOR, CA. TABLE WINE

Menu

Roasted Squash and Chestnut Bisque with Brown Butter

MERRY EDWARDS PINOT NOIR, 1998

❧

Beef Short Ribs Braised in Red Wine
with Orange Zest and Cinnamon

CLOS DU BOIS CABERNET WINEMAKER'S RESERVE, 1995

❧

Spiced Apple Fougasse with Orange Crème Fraîche

KENDALL JACKSON CHARDONNAY LATE HARVEST, 1997

Roasted Squash and Chestnut Bisque with Browned Butter

This golden soup makes a warming first course or a light supper when accompanied with a salad and crusty bread. Roasting the squash concentrates the flavor and brings out its sweetness, while chestnuts add a silky texture and richness.

1 small butternut squash, about 1½ pounds (750 g), halved and seeded
Salt and freshly ground pepper to taste
1 tablespoon olive oil
5 tablespoons unsalted butter
1 onion, thinly sliced
¼ teaspoon salt
¼ cup (2 fl oz/60 ml) dry Marsala wine
5 roasted chestnuts, peeled and chopped (see Basics)*
4 cups (32 fl oz/1 l) water
2 tablespoons heavy cream

Preheat the oven to 400°F (200°C). Sprinkle the cut sides of the squash with salt and pepper, and drizzle with olive oil. Place, cut side down, in a baking dish and bake until tender, 45 to 50 minutes. Let cool and scoop the squash out of the skin.

In a large, heavy saucepan, melt 2 tablespoons of the butter over medium-low heat and sauté the onion with the salt for 10 minutes. Add the Marsala and cook until reduced to a glaze. Add the squash, chestnuts, and water and simmer for 30 minutes. Stir in the cream. Transfer to a blender or food processor and purée until smooth. Return to the saucepan and season with salt and pepper to taste.

In a small, heavy saucepan over medium heat, melt the remaining 3 tablespoons butter and cook until browned. Immediately remove from heat and let cool slightly.

Ladle the soup into shallow bowls, drizzle each serving with brown butter, and serve immediately. *Makes 6 servings*

*Whole chestnuts are found in specialty foods markets in the fall and winter. You can also purchase peeled chestnuts.

merryedwards.com

Beef Short Ribs Braised in Red Wine with Orange Zest and Cinnamon

This hearty, simple-to-prepare dish is perfect for a dinner party on a winter evening. Have your butcher crack the ribs into 2-inch pieces. Serve with noodles or mashed potatoes and fresh crusty bread to mop up the richly flavored sauce.

2 tablespoons canola oil
2 pounds (1 kg) lean beef short ribs, 2 inches (5 cm), and trimmed
Salt and freshly ground pepper to taste
2 carrots, peeled and diced
1 onion, diced
2 cups (16 fl oz/500 ml) dry red wine
1 cinnamon stick
Zest of 1 orange, cut into wide strips
1 ancho chili, seeded and toasted in a hot, dry pan
2 cups (16 fl oz/500 ml) beef stock (see Basics) or canned low-salt beef broth

In a Dutch oven or large flameproof casserole, heat the oil over high heat until almost smoking. Add the ribs, season with salt and pepper, and brown on both sides. Transfer to a plate.

Reduce heat to medium-high and stir in the carrots, onion, and a pinch of salt; cook until the vegetables are just beginning to brown. Pour in the wine and stir to scrape up any browned bits from the bottom of the pan. Stir in the cinnamon stick, orange zest, and chili. Reduce heat to medium and boil to reduce the wine by half. Add the ribs, stock or broth, and water to cover the ribs by 1 inch (2.5 cm). Bring to a simmer and cover with a round of parchment paper. Cover, reduce heat to very low, and cook for 2 hours, or until the meat is very tender. Or, bake in a preheated 300°F (150°C) oven for 2 hours.

Using a slotted spoon, transfer the meat and vegetables to 6 warmed plates. Spoon the sauce over and serve immediately.   *Makes 6 servings*

Applewood Inn & Restaurant

SPICED APPLE FOUGASSE WITH ORANGE CRÈME FRAÎCHE

In this sweet version of the classic Provençal flat bread, apples are flavored with a hint of cardamom and topped with crème fraîche.

1 sheet thawed frozen puff pastry

1 egg yolk

1 tablespoon orange-blossom water

Powdered sugar for dusting

1 tablespoon unsalted butter

3 tart apples, such as Fuji, Gala, or Granny Smith, peeled, cored, and cut into
   ½-inch (12-mm) dice

¼ teaspoon ground cardamom

¼ teaspoon ground pepper

1 tablespoon honey

Orange Crème Fraîche (recipe follows)

❧ Preheat the oven to 450°F (230°C). Line a baking sheet with parchment paper.

❧ On a lightly floured surface, roll the pastry out to a 10-by-12-inch (25-by-30.5-cm) rectangle. Cut in half lengthwise, then cut each piece crosswise into thirds. Place on the prepared pan. Cut 3 short diagonal slits in the center of each pastry.

❧ In a small bowl, whisk the egg yolk and orange-blossom water together. Lightly brush the mixture over the pastry. Refrigerate for 30 minutes.

❧ Bake for 12 minutes, or until puffy and golden brown. Remove from the oven and dust with powdered sugar.

❧ In a large frying pan, melt the butter over medium-high heat and sauté the apples, cardamom, and pepper until the apples are tender and just beginning to brown, about 15 minutes. Remove from heat and stir in the honey.

❧ Place a mound of apples in the center of each of 6 plates. Top each mound of apples with a generous spoonful of crème fraîche and a puff pastry top.

Makes 6 servings

Orange Crème Fraîche

¼ cup (2 oz/60 g) crème fraîche*

2 tablespoons sugar

1 tablespoon orange-blossom water

1 teaspoon orange extract

In a medium bowl, combine all the ingredients and beat until soft peaks form. Refrigerate until ready to use.   *Makes about ⅓ cup*

*Crème fraîche can be found in specialty foods stores and some grocery stores. To make crème fraîche at home, see Basics.

JUSTINA SELINGER

Wine is constant proof that God loves us
and loves to see us happy.

—BENJAMIN FRANKLIN

Auberge du Soleil

Rutherford, California

Tucked away in a thirty-three-acre olive grove on the slopes of Rutherford Hill is Napa Valley's most luxurious inn. What began twenty years ago as Claude Rouas' fine California-French restaurant, became Auberge du Soleil—"Inn of the Sun"—an elegant resort where guests come to rejuvenate in an atmosphere of peace and pampering.

Each of the Auberge's elegant Mediterranean-style suites has an open fireplace and private terrace with magnificent views. Spacious and understated, the elegant rooms are designed with the highest level of personal comfort in mind. The extravagant Spa du Soleil was built for the exclusive use of Auberge guests and has an innovative menu of body and facial treatments that use grapes, herbs, flowers, olives, muds, and minerals. Other delights include the inn's swimming pool, wooden sunning deck, and Jacuzzi. A member of the prestigious Relais & Chateaux Association since 1988, Auberge du Soleil is a perfect home base for visiting nearby museums, art galleries, shops, and the more than 200 acclaimed Napa Valley wineries.

Set amid the inn's grounds is the Olive Grove Sculpture Gallery, an open-air gallery with more than 75 large-scale figurative and abstract works by forty California sculptors working in bronze, steel, ceramic, stone, and wood. Here meandering paths, mortar-less stone walls, a flowing stream, and olive trees provide contrast between art and nature, which intensifies the appreciation of both.

Each evening, chef Richard Reddington's extraordinary cooking is served in the restaurant, with its cedar columns, timbered ceiling, crackling fireplace, and French doors that open out to the gorgeous wine valley below. Executive chef Reddington has cooked at some of the best restaurants in San Francisco, New York, Los Angeles, and Paris, and his seasonally inspired menus blend subtle French flavors and bolder Mediterranean influences to highlight the agricultural riches of Napa Valley. The restaurant's extensive international wine list features the finest wines from nearby vineyards. A lighter menu is served in the bar, a casual setting with a lovely vine-covered outdoor terrace. Chef Richard Reddington created the following recipes.

Cakebread Cellars

NAPA VALLEY
Cabernet Sauvignon
1998

ALCOHOL 14.1% BY VOLUME

1997
NAPA VALLEY
CABERNET SAUVIGNON
RESERVE
UNFILTERED
ROBERT MONDAVI WINERY
ALCOHOL 14.5% BY VOLUME

1997
PETER MICHAEL
WINERY
'LES PAVOTS'

79% CABERNET SAUVIGNON, 12% MERLOT, 9% CABERNET FRANC
FROM KNIGHTS VALLEY ◆ ALCOHOL 14.5% BY VOLUME
ESTATE BOTTLED BY PETER MICHAEL • CALISTOGA, CALIFORNIA

JOSEPH PHELPS
VIN du MISTRAL
NAPA VALLEY
Syrah

A RED TABLE WINE   PRODUCED AND BOTTLED BY
JOSEPH PHELPS VINEYARDS   ST. HELENA, CALIFORNIA

Collector's Edition
Beaulieu Vineyard.
SINCE BV 1900
GEORGES DE LATOUR
Private Reserve
CABERNET SAUVIGNON
NAPA VALLEY
1997

PRODUCED & BOTTLED BY BEAULIEU VINEYARD
RUTHERFORD, CALIFORNIA

ST SUPERY
1998
Cabernet Franc
DOLLARHIDE RANCH
NAPA VALLEY

13% ALCOHOL BY VOLUME · RUTHERFORD CA 94573 USA · BW5427 750ML
VINS BLANC AND CELLARED, PRODUCED AND BOTTLED BY ST SUPERY VINEYARDS AND WINERY

GRGICH HILLS
Violetta
Napa Valley Table Wine
LATE HARVEST
1995

1999
HONIG
NAPA VALLEY
SAUVIGNON BLANC
RUTHERFORD
ALC 13.9% BY VOL.

RESERVE   RESERVE   RESERVE

NAPA VALLEY
Silverado
VINEYARDS
CABERNET SAUVIGNON
1998

Chandon
Blanc de Noirs 1998
Sparkling Wine
is a unique blend of

CARNEROS
BLANC DE NOIRS   CHANDON

89% Pinot Noir
9% Pinot Meunier and
2% Chardonnay

750 ALC. 12% BY VOL.   SPARKLING WINE

LIBRARY SELECTION
ESTATE GROWN
Trefethen
1995
NAPA VALLEY
CHARDONNAY

ALC. 13% BY VOL.

Oakville
MINER
NAPA VALLEY CABERNET SAUVIGNON
1998

ANDRETTI

1997
NAPA VALLEY CABERNET SAUVIGNON

ALCOHOL 14.1% BY VOLUME

Heitz Cellar

1999
NAPA VALLEY
CHARDONNAY
ALCOHOL 13.5% BY VOLUME
PRODUCED AND BOTTLED IN OUR CELLAR BY
HEITZ WINE CELLARS
ST. HELENA, CALIFORNIA, U.S.A.

STAGLIN FAMILY
VINEYARD
CABERNET SAUVIGNON
RUTHERFORD, NAPA VALLEY
1997

PRODUCED & BOTTLED BY STAGLIN FAMILY VINEYARD, OAKVILLE, CA 1.5L ALC. 13.8% BY VOL
"WINGED WOMAN WALKING" SCULPTURE BY STEPHEN DE STAEBLER

RUTHERFORD
HILL
1999
NAPA VALLEY
SAUVIGNON BLANC
JULIANA VINEYARDS
ALCOHOL 13.5% BY VOLUME

Menu

Sautéed Scallops with Cauliflower, Capers,
Golden Raisins, and Toasted Almonds

HONIG RESERVE SAUVIGNON BLANC, 1998 OR 1999

❧

Duck Breasts with Butternut Squash,
Brussels Sprouts Leaves, and Chestnut-Sage Sauce

ANDERSON'S CONN VALLEY PINOT NOIR VALHALLA VINEYARD, 1997

❧

Warm Chocolate Gâteaux with Caramel-Banana Ice Cream

GRGICH HILLS VIOLETTA, 1995

SAUTÉED SCALLOPS WITH CAULIFLOWER, CAPERS, GOLDEN RAISINS, AND TOASTED ALMONDS

This Spanish-inspired recipe pairs delicate golden scallops with a delightful cauliflower ragout to make a perfectly balanced dish. Enjoy with a glass of chilled Sauvignon Blanc.

½ cup (4 fl oz/125 ml) balsamic vinegar
¼ cup (1½ oz/45 g) golden raisins
1 cauliflower, cut into florets
½ cup (4 fl oz/125 ml) heavy cream or milk
3 tablespoons unsalted butter
Salt and freshly ground pepper to taste
¼ cup (2 oz/60 g) capers
¼ cup (1 oz/30 g) slivered almonds, toasted (see Basics)
2 tablespoons chopped fresh flat-leaf parsley
2 tablespoons extra-virgin olive oil, plus more for drizzling
12 sea scallops

In a small saucepan, boil the balsamic vinegar until reduced by half. Let cool, then transfer to a plastic squeeze bottle. Meanwhile, soak the raisins in warm water to cover for 15 minutes. Drain.

Cook the florets in salted boiling water for 60 seconds. Drain and rinse under cold water. Reserve 1 cup (2 oz/60 g) of the florets.

In a medium saucepan, combine the remaining florets and the cream. Simmer over medium-low heat for 8 minutes, or until tender. Transfer to a blender or food processor and purée until smooth. Set aside and keep warm.

To make the ragout: In a medium frying pan, melt the butter over medium-high heat and cook just until it begins to brown. Add the reserved cauliflower and sauté for 1 minute. Season with salt and pepper and stir in the capers, almonds, raisins, and parsley. Remove from heat.

In a large frying pan, heat the olive oil over medium-high heat until almost smoking. Pat the scallops dry, sprinkle with salt and pepper, and sauté for 1 minute, or until golden on one side. Turn and cook 1 minute more, or until browned on the second side but still slightly translucent in the center. (They will continue to cook after being removed from heat.)

Spoon a small circle of cauliflower purée in the center of each of 4 warmed plates. Spoon the ragout over and top with 3 scallops. Squeeze dots and lines of the balsamic reduction decoratively around each plate. Drizzle with olive oil and serve immediately.

Makes 4 servings

Auberge du Soleil

Duck Breasts with Butternut Squash, Brussels Sprouts Leaves, and Chestnut-Sage Sauce

Rich autumn flavors combine in this robust dish, which even Brussels sprouts haters will love. Blanching tenderizes the sprouts and makes them less bitter.

2 small butternut squash, halved and seeded
6 tablespoons (3 oz/90 g) unsalted butter at room temperature
Salt and freshly ground pepper to taste
7 or 8 Brussels sprouts, cored, leaves removed
4 boneless duck breast halves, skin intact
4 ounces (125 g) chanterelles or other wild mushrooms, thinly sliced
6 roasted chestnuts, peeled and finely chopped (see Basics)*
1 tablespoon minced fresh sage
½ cup (4 fl oz/125 ml) chicken stock (see Basics) or canned low-salt chicken
   broth
Freshly cracked pepper to taste

Preheat the oven to 350°F (180°C). Rub the cut sides of 1 squash with 1 tablespoon of the butter, sprinkle with salt and pepper, and place, cut side down, in a baking dish. Bake for 50 to 60 minutes, or until soft. Let cool and scoop out the flesh. In a food processor, combine the squash and 3 tablespoons of the butter. Purée until smooth. Season with salt and pepper. Transfer to a medium saucepan.

Cook the Brussels sprouts leaves in salted boiling water for 2 to 3 minutes, or until tender. Drain and rinse under cold water.

Using a sharp knife, peel the remaining squash and cut the flesh into ¼-inch (6-mm) dice.

Score a crisscross pattern in the skin of the duck breasts with a sharp knife, and sprinkle with salt and pepper. In a large frying pan, cook the duck breasts, skin side down, over low heat for 7 to 8 minutes, or until crispy and golden brown. Pour off the fat. Turn the breasts over and cook for 2 to 3 minutes for medium rare. Transfer to a cutting board, skin side up, and loosely cover with aluminum foil.

In a large frying pan, melt 1 tablespoon of the butter over medium-high heat and sauté the diced squash and mushrooms until the squash is tender but firm. Stir in the Brussels sprouts leaves and salt and pepper to taste.

In the same pan used to cook the duck breasts, melt the remaining 1 tablespoon butter over medium-high heat and cook the chestnuts and sage until the butter just begins to brown. Add the stock or broth, stirring to scrape up any browned bits from the bottom of the pan. Cook to reduce the liquid by half. Swirl in the remaining 1 tablespoon butter.

Warm the squash purée and spoon it onto each of 4 plates. Cut the duck breasts, skin side down, into thin lengthwise slices. Fan the slices over the purée. Scatter the diced butternut squash and mushrooms around the purée. Spoon the sauce around the plate. Sprinkle the pepper over the duck and serve immediately.

Makes 4 servings

*Whole chestnuts are found in specialty foods markets in the fall and winter. You can also purchase peeled chestnuts.

Warm Chocolate Gâteaux with Caramel-Banana Ice Cream

Individual chocolate cakes with a molten center and an exquisite deep chocolate flavor. If you prefer, serve the cakes with purchased vanilla ice cream.

½ cup (4 oz/125 g) unsalted butter

4 ounces (125 g) bittersweet chocolate, chopped

2 whole eggs

1 egg yolk

¾ cup (6 oz/185 g) sugar

½ cup (2½ oz/75 g) all-purpose flour

1½ tablespoons unsweetened cocoa powder

½ teaspoon baking powder

Caramel-Banana Ice Cream (recipe follows)

Preheat the oven to 300°F (150°C). Butter four 8-ounce (250-ml) ramekins.

In a small, heavy saucepan, melt the butter and chocolate together over low heat.

Using an electric mixer on high speed, beat the eggs, egg yolk, and sugar together until pale and nearly doubled in volume. Fold in the chocolate mixture until well blended.

In a medium bowl, combine the flour, cocoa powder, and baking powder. Stir well. Fold into the chocolate mixture. Pour the batter evenly into the prepared ramekins and bake for 20 to 25 minutes, or until a skewer inserted in the center of the cakes comes out almost clean. Remove from the oven and let cool slightly. Invert onto individual plates and serve with a scoop of ice cream. *Makes 4 individual cakes*

Caramel-Banana Ice Cream

1 cup (8 fl oz/250 ml) milk

1 cup (8 fl oz/250 ml) heavy cream

⅓ cup (3 oz/90 g) plus ½ cup (4 oz/125 g) sugar

3 egg yolks

2 very ripe bananas, mashed

In a small saucepan, combine the milk, ½ cup (4 fl oz/125 ml) of the cream, and the ⅓ cup (3 oz/90 g) sugar. Stir over medium heat to dissolve the sugar, and cook until almost boiling. Remove from heat.

In a medium bowl, whisk the egg yolks until pale. Gradually whisk in half of the hot milk mixture. Return to the saucepan and cook over medium heat, stirring constantly, until thickened, about 3 minutes. Do not boil. Remove from heat, let cool, cover, and refrigerate for 2 hours or more to chill.

In a medium, heavy saucepan, cook the ½ cup (4 oz/125 g) sugar over medium heat to a deep golden brown. Gradually stir in the remaining ½ cup (4 fl oz/125 ml) cream. Bring to a boil and stir in the banana purée. Remove from heat and stir into the chilled custard. Freeze in an ice cream maker according to the manufacturer's instructions.   *Makes 4 servings*

mt. St. Helena

EARL THOLLANDER

EARL THOLLANDER

Making good wine is a skill, fine wine an art.

—ROBERT MONDAVI

Belhurst Castle

Geneva, New York

Entering by way of an impressive port-a-cochere and leaded glass French doors, Belhurst Castle guests are swept up in a romance of richly carved hardwoods, mosaic-tiled gas fireplaces, cathedral ceilings, and views over deep blue water of a glacier-carved lake.

Built over a four year period beginning in 1885, Belhurst Castle was the dream of Carrie Harron Collins, a descendent of Henry Clay. The Collins' family home was sold in 1932, and the immense red Medina stone structure became a speakeasy and gambling casino, with gaming rooms upstairs until the early 1950s. Next serving as a restaurant before being converted to a restaurant with guest rooms upstairs, the property was purchased in 1992 by the Reeder family, who have handsomely restored the property. Listed on the National Register of Historic Places, romantic tales still persist about secret tunnels and treasures hidden in the walls and buried on Belhurst's twenty acres of parklike grounds. Guests stay in rooms and suites decorated with antique furnishings and old prints and enjoy quiet strolls through the grounds down to the shores of beautiful Seneca Lake.

Just a short drive away are the acclaimed wineries and tasting rooms of the Fingerlakes. Water skiing, fishing, golf, tennis, summer concerts and theater, museum visits, thoroughbred and auto racing, and spectacular fall foliage viewing are highlights of summer and fall pursuits, while snow skiing and ice skating are enjoyed during the winter.

At the Belhurst restaurant, dinner is by candlelight and served in six lovely rooms of the house, as well as on the covered veranda overlooking Seneca Lake, "lake trout capital of the world." Executive chef Casey Belile's seasonal menus feature produce from local farmers and the finest regional ingredients. The wine list, a recipient of *Wine Spectator* magazine's Award of Excellence for six consecutive years, features selections from outstanding Fingerlake wineries. Chef Casey Belile created the following dinner menu for Menus and Music.

Menu

Trout Cakes with Chipotle Sauce

GOOSE WATCH VILLARD BLANC

Venison Chops with Mushroom Pesto and
Root-Vegetable Pancakes

HERON HILL ECLIPSE

Panna Cotta

CHATEAU FRANK ROSE CHAMPAGNE

TROUT CAKES WITH CHIPOTLE SAUCE

The mild flavors of trout and crab are enlivened with a smoky chipotle sauce. If trout is unavailable, salmon is also delicious in this recipe. Make the chipotle sauce ahead so the flavors have a chance to blend.

2 tablespoons mayonnaise
1 egg, lightly beaten
½ teaspoon dry mustard
½ teaspoon Old Bay seasoning
2 green onions, white part only, finely chopped
1 tablespoon minced fresh cilantro
2 tablespoons fresh bread crumbs
5 ounces (155 g) grilled or broiled trout, chilled and flaked
5 ounces (155 g) fresh lump crabmeat, picked over for shell
Flour for dredging
2 tablespoons olive oil
Chipotle Sauce (recipe follows)

➤ In a medium bowl, stir together the mayonnaise, egg, mustard, Old Bay seasoning, onion, cilantro, and bread crumbs. Gently mix in the trout and crab. Shape the mixture into 8 patties, each about 2½ inches (6 cm) in diameter. They will barely hold together. Spread the flour on a plate and lightly dredge the patties, coating evenly. Place the patties on a plate, cover, and refrigerate for at least 30 minutes.

➤ In a large frying pan, heat 1 tablespoon of the olive oil over medium-high heat and cook half of the trout cakes until golden, about 3 minutes on each side. Repeat for the remaining cakes. Arrange 2 trout cakes and a dollop of chipotle sauce on each of 4 plates and serve immediately.   *Makes 4 servings*

CHIPOTLE SAUCE

¼ cup (2 oz/60 g) mayonnaise
¼ cup (2 oz/60 g) sour cream
4 canned chipotle chilies en adobo
1 garlic clove, minced

1 teaspoon fresh lime juice
2 teaspoons chopped fresh flat-leaf parsley
2 teaspoons capers

➤ In a blender or food processor, combine all the ingredients and purée until smooth. Cover and refrigerate for 1 to 2 hours to chill.

Makes about ¾ cup

Venison Chops with Mushroom Pesto and Root-Vegetable Pancakes

Chef Casey Belile uses wild woodear mushrooms for this pesto. If venison is unavailable, use veal loin chops.

Mushroom Pesto
4 tablespoons (2 fl oz/60 ml) olive oil
8 ounces (250 g) porcini, stemmed shiitake, or cremini mushrooms, chopped
3 garlic cloves, minced
2 green onions, white part only, chopped
¼ cup (1 oz/30 g) pine nuts
¼ cup (1 oz/30 g) grated Parmesan cheese

1 tablespoon olive oil
4 venison loin chops
Salt and freshly ground pepper to taste
Root-Vegetable Pancakes (recipe follows)

To make the pesto: In a large frying pan, heat 2 tablespoons of the olive oil over medium-high heat until almost smoking. Add the mushrooms and sauté for 5 minutes, or until most of the moisture has evaporated. Add the garlic, green onions, and pine nuts and sauté for 3 minutes. In a blender or food processor, combine the mushrooms, garlic mixture, and Parmesan. Purée until smooth.

In a large frying pan, heat the olive oil over medium-high heat. Add the venison chops, sprinkle with salt and pepper, and sauté for 3 to 4 minutes on each side for medium rare.

To serve, arrange 2 pancakes on each of 4 warmed plates and place a venison chop on top. Top each chop with a dollop of mushroom pesto and serve immediately. *Makes 4 servings*

Root-Vegetable Pancakes

1 cup (5 oz/155 g) all-purpose flour
½ teaspoon salt
½ teaspoon baking powder
¼ teaspoon baking soda
¼ cup (2 fl oz/60 ml) buttermilk
¼ cup (2 fl oz/60 ml) milk
1 egg
2 tablespoons unsalted butter, melted
¼ cup (1 oz/30 g) each grated peeled parsnip, carrot, potato, and rutabaga
2 tablespoons olive oil

In a medium bowl, combine all the ingredients except the olive oil. In a large frying pan, heat 1 tablespoon of the olive oil over medium-high heat until almost smoking. Drop in ¼ cupfuls of batter to form 3 pancakes. Reduce heat to medium and cook for 2 to 3 minutes on each side, or until well browned. Transfer to a low oven to keep warm. Repeat with the remaining 1 tablespoon oil and the remaining batter. Serve warm. *Makes 4 servings*

PANNA COTTA

A perfect dessert for a dinner party, as it can be made a day or two in advance. At Belhurst Castle, this silky, eggless custard is topped with fresh raspberries or small, sweet Champagne grapes.

½ cup (4 fl oz / 125 ml) milk
1 ¼ teaspoons plain gelatin
3 tablespoons sugar
1 ½ cups (12 fl oz / 375 ml) heavy cream
1 teaspoon vanilla extract
1 cup (4 oz / 125 g) raspberries or Champagne grapes for garnish

Pour the milk into a small saucepan, place over medium-low heat, and sprinkle in the gelatin. Stir until the gelatin dissolves. Remove from heat and stir in the sugar, cream, and vanilla.

Pour into 4 shallow Champagne or martini glasses. Refrigerate for at least 6 hours. Arrange the raspberries or grapes on top and serve. *Makes 4 servings*

ALEX FONG

I cook with wine; sometimes I even add it to the food.

—W.C. FIELDS

Bernardus Lodge

Carmel Valley, California

Created in 1999 by Benardus Pon of Bernardus Winery and Vineyards, this epicurean destination offers sumptuous rooms and suites, Marinus restaurant, a full-service spa and salon, and resort activities. Ben Pon is an enthusiastic *bon vivant* who once was a race car driver for Porsche, racing six times in Le Mans, and an athlete for Holland in skeet shooting during the 1972 Olympics. Pon's passion for the best has fueled his dream of making a Carmel Valley red wine equal to the finest from Bordeaux and his desire to create Bernardus Lodge.

Guests can spend their days rejuvenating at the spa or relaxing around the pool, playing tennis, or unwinding over games of croquet and boccie ball. Nearby are acclaimed wineries in one of California's most beautiful wine making regions, ten championship golf courses, hiking and horseback riding on more than 4,000 acres of mountain trails, and the Monterey Bay Aquarium. Both Bernardus Lodge and Marinus restaurant are recipients of Mobil Travel Guide's Four-Star award.

Marinus restaurant showcases chef Cal Stamenov's sophisticated menu of California-French cuisine. Chef Stamenov has worked at some of the top restaurants in France, Monaco, and the United States. His cooking is based on classic French technique and makes creative use of fresh local produce, seafood from Monterey Bay, and fresh herbs and vegetables gathered from an on-site chef's garden. Wine Director Mark Jensen developed the restaurant's extensive cellar and will gladly pair wines with each course of the menu. The wine list has received *Wine Spectator* magazine's Best of Award of Excellence, and Jensen and chef Stamenov are working together to create a series of wine and food pairing classes. A stunning twelve-foot limestone fireplace is a focal point of the restaurant and there is an inviting outdoor terrace for dining al fresco. Wickets, the resort's bar and bistro, offers French country cuisine and live jazz on the weekends. Chef Cal Stamenov created the following recipes and presented them to Menus and Music.

CHATEAU CHRISTINA
Monterey County
Pinot Noir
1997
Francioni Vineyard
PRODUCED AND BOTTLED BY JOYCE VINEYARDS, CARMEL VALLEY, CA
750 ML • ALCOHOL 13.9% BY VOLUME

GEORIS
quand i tât c'est   po tot l'monde
SAUVIGNON
BLANC
Monterey
1999
Produced and Bottled by Georis Winery
Carmel Valley, California . alcohol 13% by volume

TALBOTT
1998
Chardonnay
SLEEPY HOLLOW VINEYARD
MONTEREY WHITE TABLE WINE
PRODUCED & BOTTLED BY ROBERT TALBOTT VINEYARDS
GONZALES, CA. USA

1999
BARREL AGED
CHATEAU
JULIEN
MONTEREY COUNTY
Cabernet Sauvignon
ALC. 13.2% BY VOL.

GALANTE
VINEYARDS
RED ROSE HILL
1998 CARMEL VALLEY
Cabernet Sauvignon
ESTATE BOTTLED
ALC. 12.5% BY VOL. • 750ML

1998
BARREL AGED
CHATEAU
JULIEN
MONTEREY COUNTY
Merlot
ALC. 13.8% BY VOL.

B E R N A R D U S
1 9 9 9
Monterey County
SAUVIGNON
BLANC
PRODUCED AND BOTTLED BY BERNARDUS WINERY
CARMEL VALLEY, CALIFORNIA. ALCOHOL 13.1% BY VOLUME

GEORIS
quand i tât c'est   po tot l'monde
ESTATE   BOTTLED
1996
CABERNET
SAUVIGNON
Carmel Valley
grown, produced and bottled by Georis Winery
Carmel Valley, California alcohol 13.0% by volume

B E R N A R D U S
1 9 9 6
MARINUS
Carmel Valley Red Wine
ESTATE GROWN AND BOTTLED
ALCOHOL 13.2% BY VOLUME

TALBOTT
1997 VINTAGE
DIAMOND T ESTATE
MONTEREY CHARDONNAY TABLE WINE
ESTATE GROWN, PRODUCED & BOTTLED BY
ROBERT TALBOTT, GONZALES, CA, USA

JOULLIAN
CARMEL VALLEY
CABERNET SAUVIGNON
1995
ESTATE GROWN, PRODUCED & BOTTLED BY JOULLIAN VINEYARDS LTD. © 1998
CARMEL VALLEY, CALIFORNIA • ALCOHOL 13% BY VOLUME

Dances On Your Palate
DURNEY
VINEYARDS
1992
Estate Bottled
CARMEL VALLEY
CABERNET SAUVIGNON
750 ml   Product of U.S.A.   Alc. 14.5% by Vol.
PRIVATE RESERVE

Menu

Tuna Tartare with Ginger Dressing

BERNARDUS SAUVIGNON BLANC, 1999

❧

Coriander and Mustard Seed—Crusted Salmon

GALANTE CABERNET SAUVIGNON BLACK JACK PASTURE, 1997

❧

Roasted Chestnut Soufflé with Spiced Cider Drink

CAROL PARKER

Excellent wine generates enthusiasm.
And whatever you do with enthusiasm
is generally successful.

—PHILLIPPE DE ROTHSCHILD, FRENCH VINTNER

TUNA TARTARE WITH GINGER DRESSING

*This elegant appetizer, flavored with tart lime and spicy ginger, is presented as a
dramatic tower at Bernardus.*

7 ounces (220 g) ahi tuna, very finely diced
½ cup peeled, seeded, and finely diced tomato (see Basics)
2 tablespoons minced shallot
2 tablespoons minced fresh chives
2 tablespoons fresh lemon juice
Salt and freshly ground pepper to taste
¼ cup (2 fl oz/60 ml) Ginger Dressing (recipe follows)
4 chervil sprigs for garnish (optional)

In a medium bowl, combine all the ingredients except the dressing and
chervil sprigs. Pool a little of the dressing in the center of each of 4 plates.
Using a knife, pull the dressing out in lines to make a sunburst shape. Using
an empty 6-ounce can of tomato paste with the top and bottom removed,
place the can on the dressing and fill it with about ½ cup (4 oz/125 g) of the
tuna. Remove the mold, leaving about a 2-inch (5-cm) tower of tuna tartare.
Garnish with a chervil sprig, if desired. Repeat to make 3 more servings.
Serve immediately. *Makes 4 servings*

GINGER DRESSING

1 egg yolk
Juice of 1 lime
1 teaspoon peeled minced fresh ginger
½ cup (4 fl oz/125 ml) olive oil
Salt to taste

In a blender, combine the egg yolk, lime juice, and ginger and purée until
smooth. With the machine running, gradually add the olive oil in a thin stream
to make an emulsified sauce. Add salt. *Makes about ½ cup (4 fl oz/125 ml)*

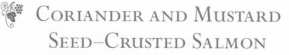

CORIANDER AND MUSTARD
SEED–CRUSTED SALMON

*Spicy salmon, mildly bitter greens, and a smooth sauce create a well-balanced dish.
If you don't have mustard oil, use 2 tablespoons canola oil whisked with ¼ teaspoon
dry mustard.*

SAUCE
6 slices bacon, chopped
4 shallots, minced
2 leeks, white part only, sliced
6 garlic cloves, minced
2 cups (15 oz/470 g) cooked white beans
Leaves from 6 thyme sprigs, chopped
Leaves from 4 lemon thyme sprigs, chopped
4 cups (32 fl oz/1 l) chicken stock (see Basics) or
    canned low-salt chicken broth
Salt and freshly ground pepper to taste

MUSTARD GREENS AND ARTICHOKES
2 lemons, halved
8 baby artichokes
2 tablespoons extra-virgin olive oil
4 garlic cloves, minced
¼ cup (2 fl oz/60 ml) water
Salt and freshly ground pepper to taste
1 bunch young mustard greens, stemmed and chopped

¼ cup (1 oz/30 g) brown mustard seeds
¼ cup (1 oz/30 g) coriander seeds
4 salmon fillets, pin bones and skin removed
Salt and freshly ground pepper to taste
2 tablespoons mustard seed oil
¼ cup (2 fl oz/60 ml) olive oil

To make the sauce: In a medium saucepan, sauté the bacon over medium
heat until lightly browned. Pour off all but 1 tablespoon of the bacon fat. Add
the shallots, leeks, and garlic and sauté for 3 to 4 minutes, or until the shallots

are translucent. Stir in the white beans, thyme, lemon thyme, and about 3 cups (24 fl oz/750 ml) of the stock or broth (enough to cover the beans), and bring to boil. Reduce heat to low and simmer for 50 to 60 minutes, or until the beans are very soft. Transfer to a blender or food processor and purée. Return to the saucepan. Add the remaining stock or broth and season with salt and pepper. Heat over medium heat. Set aside and keep warm.

To make the mustard greens and artichokes: Fill a bowl with cold water and squeeze in the juice of 1 lemon. Pull off the outer leaves of each artichoke to reach the tender inner leaves. Cut about 1 inch (2.5 cm) from the top of each artichoke and immediately rub the cut surfaces with the other 2 lemon halves to prevent the artichokes from turning brown. Trim the stem of each artichoke and rub with lemon. Halve each artichoke vertically and cut each half into 4 wedges. Squeeze the lemon halves over the artichokes and transfer them to the lemon water.

In a large, heavy saucepan, heat the olive oil over medium heat and sauté the garlic for 2 minutes, or until fragrant. Stir in the artichokes, cover, and cook for 10 minutes, stirring occasionally. Add the water and season with salt and pepper. Cover and cook for 10 minutes, stirring frequently and adding more water if the mixture seems dry. Add the mustard greens and sauté for 3 minutes, or until just wilted. Season with salt and pepper to taste. Remove from heat and keep warm.

Preheat the oven to 450°F (230°C). Put the mustard seeds and coriander seeds on a cutting board and crack them with the bottom of a small skillet or pan; transfer to a plate.

Sprinkle the fillets with salt and pepper on both sides and coat one side with the mustard-seed mixture. In a large ovenproof frying pan, heat the oils over medium-high heat. Add the salmon to the pan, coated side down, and cook for 3 to 4 minutes, or until a rich golden brown on the bottom. Turn the fillets over, transfer the pan to the oven, and roast for 3 to 4 minutes, or until the fillets are just barely translucent in the center.

To serve, spoon a circle of sauce into 4 warmed shallow soup bowls and arrange a mound of mustard greens and artichokes on top. Place a salmon fillet over the greens, crust side up, and serve immediately. *Makes 4 servings*

Roasted Chestnut Soufflé with Spiced Cider Drink

This light, flavorful soufflé and spiced cider drink harmonize perfectly. The chestnut soufflé base can be made 1 day in advance.

Soufflé Base

10 roasted chestnuts, peeled and coarsely chopped (see Basics)
1 vanilla bean, split and scraped, or 1 teaspoon vanilla extract
⅓ cup (3 oz/ 125 g) sugar
4 teaspoons Cognac or brandy

3 egg yolks
6 egg whites
3 tablespoons sugar
½ teaspoon fresh lemon juice

Preheat the oven to 350°F (180°C). To make the base: In a small saucepan, combine the chestnuts and all the remaining base ingredients. Cook for 20 minutes over medium-low heat, or until the chestnuts are soft. Transfer to a blender or food processor and purée. Cover and refrigerate for at least 2 hours or overnight.

Preheat the oven to 400°F (200°C). Coat the bottom and sides of four 8-ounce (250-ml) soufflé dishes or ramekins with butter, sprinkle with sugar, and knock to evenly coat.

In a medium bowl, beat the chestnut purée and yolks together until smooth. In a large bowl, beat the egg whites until foamy. Add the sugar and lemon juice and beat until soft peaks form. Stir one-fourth of the whites into the purée, then fold in the remaining whites. Spoon into the prepared dishes and bake for 13 minutes, or until puffed and golden but still soft in the center. Serve immediately.

Makes 4 soufflés

Spiced Cider Drink

4 cups (32 fl oz/ 1 l) apple juice
2 cinnamon sticks
4 cloves

4 long strips tangerine zest
1 teaspoon peeled minced fresh ginger
1 tablespoon honey

In a medium saucepan, combine all the ingredients and bring to a simmer over low heat. Remove from heat, cover, and let steep for at least 20 minutes. Strain and pour into cups to serve.

Makes 4 cups (32 fl oz/ 1 l)

Birchfield Manor Country Inn

Yakima, Washington

Located East of the Cascade Mountains and near some of the finest wineries on the West Coast, Birchfield Manor is renowned for its regional cooking and for its wine cellar. Built in 1910, the eleven-room brick mansion has a convivial country house atmosphere and is very much a family home.

Wil and Sandy Masset purchased Birchfield Manor in 1979 and opened their restaurant that year. Trained in Switzerland and a professional cooking instructor for more than twenty-five years, Wil Masset established Birchfield's Northwest menu with classic French influences. Today Brad Masset, Wil and Sandy's son, presides in the kitchen, while Wil concentrates on his garden, which provides herbs, edible flowers, and vegetables for the kitchen.

Birchfield's eleven comfortably furnished bedrooms overlook either the peaceful surrounding countryside or the park-like grounds that surround the inn's outdoor swimming pool. Birchfield is an ideal home base for touring local wineries, and within the Walla Walla, Tri Cities, and Yakima regions there are hundreds of acclaimed vineyards to visit. Other popular activities include flyfishing in the Yakima River, golfing, and visiting roadside stands for fresh fruits and vegetables.

Brad Masset's creatively prepared seasonal dishes are served in Birchfield's charming, casual dining room. The restaurant's wine list features outstanding wines from Yakima Valley, as well as Northwest and California wines, and you may find that your favorite winemaker is dining at the next table! Each morning guests enjoy a gourmet breakfast with breads, muffins, and pastries baked by pastry chef Greg Masset, Wil and Sandy's youngest son. Chef Brad Masset created the following dinner menu for Menus and Music.

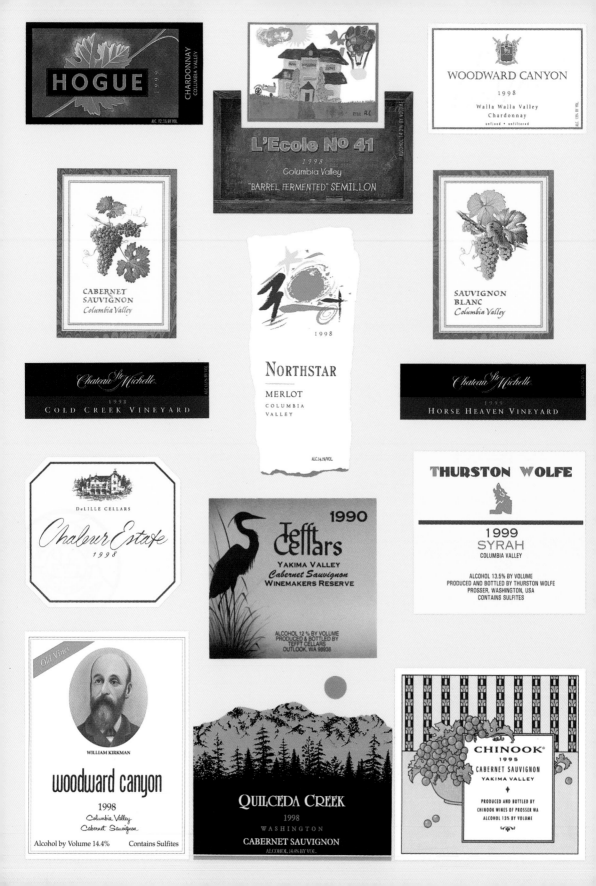

Menu

Sesame Seed–Crusted Salmon with Apple-Mango Salsa

L'Ecole Nº 41 Barrel Fermented Semillon

❧

Herbed Chèvre–Stuffed Mushroom Caps
with Lemon Thyme Croutons

Bonair Barrel Fermented Dry Riesling

❧

Baked Rack of Lamb

Apex Merlot

❧

Birchfield Pear Tart

Sesame Seed–Crusted Salmon with Apple-Mango Salsa

The delicate flavor of roasted salmon pairs beautifully with this colorful salsa. If sweet Walla Walla onions are unavailable, use Vidalias, Mauis, or Texas Sweets. Prepare the salsa a few hours before you plan to serve it so the flavors have a chance to blend.

¼ cup (1 oz / 30 g) dried bread crumbs
2 tablespoons black sesame seeds
2 tablespoons white sesame seeds
4 salmon fillets, pin bones removed
Salt and freshly ground pepper to taste
2 tablespoons olive oil
Apple-Mango Salsa (recipe follows)
4 cilantro sprigs for garnish

Preheat the oven to 350°F (180°C). In a shallow bowl, stir the bread crumbs and sesame seeds together. Sprinkle each fillet with salt and pepper and dredge in the bread crumb mixture to coat evenly.

In a large ovenproof frying pan, heat the olive oil over medium-high heat until almost smoking. Add the fillets, skin side down, and cook until golden brown on the bottom, about 2 minutes. Transfer the pan to the oven and roast for 6 to 8 minutes, or until just slightly translucent in the center. Transfer the salmon to individual plates and top with a dollop of salsa. Garnish each with a cilantro sprig and serve immediately.

Makes 4 servings

APPLE-MANGO SALSA

1 small mango, peeled and diced (see Basics)
1 Golden Delicious apple, peeled, cored, and grated
1 jalapeno chili, seeded and minced
½ poblano pepper, seeded and finely diced
2 tablespoons chopped fresh cilantro
¼ cup (1 oz / 30 g) finely diced Walla Walla onion
Salt and freshly ground pepper to taste
½ tablespoon packed brown sugar
1 tomato, peeled, seeded, and finely diced (see Basics)

In a medium bowl, combine all the ingredients and stir until blended. Set aside to let the flavors blend, or cover and refrigerate for up to 1 day.

Makes about 2 cups (8 oz / 250 g)

Birchfield Manor Country Inn

Herbed Chevre–Stuffed Mushroom Caps with Lemon Thyme Croutons

8 ounces (250 g) fresh white goat cheese at room temperature

1 tablespoon minced mixed fresh herbs, such as chives, thyme, marjoram, and chervil

½ tablespoon freshly ground pepper

1 cup (8 fl oz/250 ml) Chardonnay wine

Juice of 1 lemon

1 teaspoon salt

16 extra-large cremini mushrooms, stemmed

½ cup (4 fl oz/125 ml) extra-virgin olive oil

¼ cup (1/3 oz/10 g) minced lemon thyme

16 thin diagonal slices baguette

Paprika for sprinkling

Preheat the oven to 375°F (190°C). In a medium bowl, combine the goat cheese, herbs, and pepper. Stir until well blended.

In a medium saucepan, bring the wine, lemon juice, and salt to a boil. Reduce to a simmer, add the mushrooms, and cook for 10 minutes. Using a slotted spoon, transfer the mushrooms to a plate and let cool.

In a small frying pan, heat the olive oil over low heat. Add the lemon thyme and cook for about 3 minutes. Remove from heat and let steep until the oil cools to room temperature. Brush the bread slices lightly on both sides with the thyme-oil. Arrange the bread on a baking sheet and bake for about 10 minutes, or until golden.

Stuff the mushrooms with the goat cheese mixture and sprinkle lightly with paprika. Place on a baking sheet and bake for 10 minutes, or until heated through. Arrange the mushrooms and croutons on a warmed plate and serve.

Makes 16 stuffed mushrooms; serves 4 as an appetizer

❧ BAKED RACK OF LAMB ❧

Tender, delicious lamb spiked with a zesty marinade. Ask your butcher to "French" the rack, which means trimming the meat from the end of the bones.

MARINADE
¼ cup (2 fl oz/60 ml) thawed frozen apple juice concentrate
¼ cup (2 oz/60 g) sugar
⅓ cup (3 fl oz/80 ml) soy sauce
⅓ cup (3 oz/90 g) Dijon mustard
3 tablespoons olive oil
1 teaspoon minced garlic

2 racks of lamb
2 teaspoons freshly ground pepper

❧ Preheat the oven to 375°F (190°C). In a small bowl, combine all the marinade ingredients.

❧ Sprinkle the lamb racks all over with pepper. In a large ovenproof frying pan, brown one lamb rack at a time on all sides over medium-high heat. Brush the racks with the marinade, transfer to the oven, and roast for 7 minutes. Remove from the oven and brush again with the marinade. Continue roasting until an instant-read thermometer inserted in the center of a rack and not touching bone registers 130°F (54°C) for rare, or 140°F (60°C) for medium rare.

❧ Transfer the lamb to a warmed platter and cover loosely with aluminum foil. Let stand for 10 minutes. Cut the lamb racks into individual chops and serve immediately.   *Makes 4 servings*

BIRCHFIELD PEAR TART

Make this luscious, rich tart in the fall when pears and hazelnuts, also called filberts, are harvested.

PASTRY DOUGH

10 tablespoons (5 oz/160 g) unsalted butter at room temperature
½ cup (4 oz/125 g) sugar
1¼ cups (7 oz/220 g) all-purpose flour
1 egg, lightly beaten
1 tablespoon milk (optional)

FILLING

1 cup (8 fl oz/250 ml) late-harvest Riesling or other white dessert wine
½ cup (4 oz/125 g) unsalted butter at room temperature
½ cup (4 oz/125 g) sugar
4 ounces (125 g) almond paste, chopped into small pieces
3 tablespoons sugar
3 ripe Bartlett pears, peeled, cored, and quartered
1 egg
1 egg yolk
1 cup (4 oz/125 g) hazelnuts or almonds, finely ground
1 tablespoon flour
1 tablespoon rum or brandy

➤ To make the dough: In a medium bowl, cream the butter and sugar together until light and fluffy. Using a fork, stir in the flour and egg and mix just until the dough forms a ball; do not overmix. If the mixture is too dry, stir in the milk. Flatten the dough into a disk, cover with plastic wrap or place in a self-sealing plastic bag, and refrigerate for at least 30 minutes or overnight.

➤ Preheat the oven to 350°F (180°C). On a lightly floured work surface, roll the dough out to a 12-inch (30-cm) circle. Fit into a 10-inch (25-cm) tart pan and run the rolling pin over the top of the pan to trim the edges. Prick the pastry with a fork and refrigerate for 30 minutes.

➤ Bake the tart shell for 16 minutes, or until golden. Remove from the oven and let cool on a wire rack for 10 minutes.

➤ In a medium saucepan, combine the wine and sugar. Bring to a boil, stirring to dissolve the sugar. Reduce heat to just below a simmer. Gently add the pears to the wine and cook for 8 minutes, or until soft when pierced. Remove from heat and drain.

🍃 To make the filling: Using an electric mixer, beat the butter, sugar, and almond paste until smooth, 3 to 5 minutes. Beat in the egg, egg yolk, nuts, flour, and rum or brandy until light and fluffy.

🍃 Spread the filling evenly in the pastry shell. Cut the pears into slices, ¼ inch (6 mm) thick. Overlap the slices in concentric circles over the filling. Bake for 30 to 35 minutes, or until a skewer inserted in the center comes out almost clean. Let the tart cool completely before serving.

Makes one 10-inch (25-cm) tart

BILL BRENNEN

Wine is as good as life to a man, if it be drunk moderately; what is life then to a man that is without wine? For it was made to make men glad. Wine measurably drunk, and in season, bringeth gladness of the heart, and cheerfulness of the mind. ECCLESIASTES, 31:27-28

Birchfield Manor Country Inn

Clifton
The Country Inn & Estate
Charlottesville, Virginia

ocated in the heart of Virginia wine country and just minutes from Monticello, this historic inn is set in a tranquil forty-acre estate and offers Southern hospitality at its best. The manor house was built in 1799 by Thomas Mann Randolph, a governor of Virginia, member of the United States Congress, and husband of Thomas Jefferson's beloved daughter, Martha. A fine example of Federal and Colonial revival style architecture, the structure's south wing was enlarged and a second story added during the 1920s. Clifton remained a private residence until 1985 when it was restored by Mitch and Emily Willey and opened as an elegant country inn. Clifton's restaurant opened in 1991, and the inn has been awarded four stars by the Mobil Travel Guide and four diamonds by the American Automobile Association.

Clifton's antique-appointed rooms and suites overlook the inn's expansive lawns, gardens, and private lake. Comfortable sofas, fireplaces, and fresh flowers are found throughout the house. Leisurely breakfasts are taken on the veranda and afternoon teas enjoyed in the drawing room or library. Guests spend their days enjoying Clifton's clay tennis court, swimming pool with waterfall, and croquet lawns, or venture further afield to explore Virginia wine country. Nearby are Presidential homes and estates including Monticello, Thomas Jefferson's family home, and Montpelier, home of James and Dolly Madison. Jefferson's most imposing architectural accomplishment, the University of Virginia, is only five miles away.

Each evening Clifton's chef hosts a wine reception and previews the dinner menu. Thomas Jefferson himself would love the restaurant's imaginative seasonal dishes that highlight fresh regional ingredients and its extensive wine list. In midsummer on the pool deck under the stars, fine cuisine and wine share the stage with live jazz at Clifton's annual celebration, "Hot Nights and Cool Jazz." Clifton's mahogany-paneled wine cellar holds over 5,000 bottles and its international wine list has received *Wine Spectator* magazine's Award of Excellence for four consecutive years. So enjoy a glass of wine from a local vineyard and toast our third president for instilling respect for that most American of ideals: the pursuit of happiness.

Menu

Chicken and Andouille Sausage Gumbo

HORTON CELLARS VIOGNIER, 1998 OR 1999

❧

Jerk Pork Tenderloin with
Garlic Mashed Potatoes and Mango Chutney

HORTON CELLARS SYRAH, 1998

❧

Bananas Foster

WHITE HALL VINEYARD SOLITERRE, 2000

FREDERICK NICHOLS, COLLECTION OF DR. & MRS. ROBERT BARNES

Good wine is a necessity of life.

—THOMAS JEFFERSON

Chicken and Andouille Sausage Gumbo

Thick, meaty, and suffused with spice, this gumbo makes a delicious first course to serve with corn bread.

Roux
½ cup (4 fl oz / 125 ml) canola oil, olive oil, or melted butter
½ cup (2½ oz / 75 g) flour

Salt to taste
½ tablespoon cayenne pepper
1 tablespoon dried oregano
1 tablespoon dried thyme
1 tablespoon chopped fresh flat leaf parsley
1½ tablespoons filé powder*

Soup
2 celery stalks, chopped
1 onion, chopped
1 large green bell pepper, seeded, deribbed, and chopped
3 boneless, skinless chicken breast halves, cut into ½-inch (12-mm) cubes
8 ounces (250 g) andouille sausage,** cut into slices ½ inch (12 mm) thick
4 cups (32 fl oz / 1 l) chicken stock (see Basics) or
   canned low-salt chicken broth

To make the roux: In a large heavy saucepan, heat the oil or butter over medium heat. Using a wooden spoon, stir in the flour and cook, stirring constantly, until the mixture is the color of peanut butter, about 30 minutes. Do not allow it to burn, or the dish will have a scorched taste. In a small bowl, combine all the seasonings and stir to blend. Turn off the heat and carefully stir the seasonings into the very hot roux. Stir in the celery, onion, bell pepper, chicken, and sausage, then the stock or broth. Return to medium heat and cook until thick. Serve hot, with corn bread. *Makes 6 servings*

*Filé powder is a thickening agent made from the leaves of the sassafras tree. Look for it in the spice section of your grocery store.

**Andouille Sausage is a smoked, spicy pork sausage basted with cane sugar.

Clifton, The Country Inn

Jerk Pork Tenderloin with Garlic Mashed Potatoes and Mango Chutney

Flavorful tender pork and a refreshing chutney on a bed of comforting mashed potatoes.

½ cup (4 oz/125 g) jerk seasoning* (see Basics)
2 pork tenderloins, about 1 pound (16 oz/500 g) each
½ cup (4 fl oz/125 ml) Worcestershire sauce

Garlic Mashed Potatoes

6 large white potatoes, peeled
4 tablespoons (2 oz/60 g) unsalted butter
1 cup (16 fl oz/500 ml) heavy (whipping) cream or milk
2 small garlic cloves, minced
Salt and freshly ground pepper to taste

Mango Chutney (recipe follows)

Preheat the oven to 350°F (180°C). Spread the jerk seasoning on a plate and roll the tenderloins in it to coat evenly. Transfer the tenderloins to a baking dish and pour in the Worcestershire and enough water to cover the meat. Cover with aluminum foil and bake for 1 hour, or until fork tender. Transfer the pork to a plate, cover loosely with foil and let rest for 10 minutes.

About 20 minutes before the pork is done, make the mashed potatoes. Cook the potatoes in salted boiling water for 15 to 20 minutes, or until tender. Drain.

In a small saucepan, melt the butter over medium-low heat. Add the cream or milk and garlic and cook at a low simmer for 10 minutes. Mash the potatoes and stir in the cream mixture to the desired consistency. Season with salt and pepper. Set aside and keep warm.

To serve, place a mound of mashed potatoes in the center of each of 6 warmed plates. Arrange the sliced tenderloin around the potatoes and top the meat with the chutney; serve immediately.   *Makes 6 servings*

*Look for jerk seasoning in the supermarket, order it by mail from Penzey's (see Resources), or make your own (see Basics).

Clifton, The Country Inn

MANGO CHUTNEY

2 mangos, peeled and diced (see Basics)

1 small red onion, finely diced

1 garlic clove, minced

1 teaspoon cloves

1 teaspoon ground ginger

1 teaspoon salt

½ teaspoon ground white pepper

¼ cup (2 fl oz / 60 ml) red wine vinegar

2 teaspoons canola oil

In a heavy, medium saucepan, combine all the ingredients and bring to a simmer over medium heat. Cook for 10 to 15 minutes, or until thickened. Let cool to room temperature.   *Makes about 2 cups (16 fl oz / 500 ml)*

 Bananas Foster

In 1951, a chef at the legendary Brennan's restaurant in New Orleans created a banana dish in honor of one of the restaurant's loyal patrons, Richard Foster. Since then, the dessert has become synonymous with the South.

3 bananas, peeled and halved crosswise
½ cup (4 oz/125 g) unsalted butter
½ cup (3½ oz/105 g) packed brown sugar
¼ cup (2 fl oz/60 ml) dark rum
¼ cup (2 fl oz/60 ml) Galliano* liqueur
¼ teaspoon salt
1 quart vanilla bean ice cream

❧ Cut the banana pieces in half lengthwise. In a large frying pan, combine the butter, brown sugar, and salt. Cook over medium heat until blended and bubbling. Add the bananas and sauté for about 1 minute. Remove from heat and carefully stir in the rum and Galliano. Return to medium heat and cook for 3 or 4 minutes.

❧ To serve, place a large scoop of ice cream in each of 6 shallow bowls. Arrange 2 banana pieces on top, pour the sauce over, and serve immediately.

Makes 6 servings

*Galliano is an anise-flavored liqueur.

Gaige House Inn

Glen Ellen, California

Owners Ken Burnet and Greg Nemrow have transformed an 1890 Queen Anne-Italianate building into a luxuriously romantic inn with a restful mix of antiques, modern art, and Asian-inspired influences. Fresh, modern, and comfortable, the sophisticated inn is a perfect homebase for a wine country escape.

Located in the wooded hamlet of Glen Ellen, Gaige House is surrounded by an acre and a half of lovely gardens, with an in-season heated pool, Jacuzzi, and redwood sundeck. The two-story main house has six spacious guest rooms, a sunny breakfast room, a large welcoming kitchen, and a comfortable parlor. The garden annex has five rooms near the swimming pool, and a separate building houses two spectacular suites, one overlooking Calabazas Creek. Spa appointments for services such as massage, wraps, and reflexology are available with a simple call to the concierge. Gaige House received Four Stars from the Mobil Travel Guide in 2001 and was rated the number one bed and breakfast for 2000 by *Travel & Leisure* magazine.

Within minutes of the inn are many world-class wineries, the five hundred acre Bouverie Wildflower Preserve, and Jack London State Park, with its miles of oak-shaded trails and museum dedicated to the writer. Guests also enjoy horseback rides, picnics, hot air balloon rides, watching a Glen Ellen olive press churn out small batches of extra-virgin olive oil, and visiting the nearby historic town of Sonoma. At the end of the day, Gaige House guests assemble in the parlor for a casual wine tasting, with appetizers and a selection of regional vintages. For dinner, it's just a short walk to the many outstanding restaurants of Glen Ellen.

Breakfasts at Gaige House are served in courses and are outrageously good. Chef Charles Holmes, who has worked with great chefs such as Gary Danko and Phillipe Jeanty, brings the style and creativity usually associated with dinner to breakfast. He says that each season "is like a new palette from which to create. I strive to present each ingredient clearly yet creatively." Chef Holmes created the following recipes and presented them to Menus and Music.

CHARLES BECK

The flavor of wine is like delicate poetry.
—LOUIS PASTEUR

Breakfast Menu

California Sunshine

❧

Oatmeal with Fresh Fruit and Currants

❧

Cinnamon-Raspberry Muffins

❧

Quince with Star Anise

CALIFORNIA SUNSHINE

Chef Charles Holmes' decorative first course is also delicious without the orange rind pedestals.

6 oranges
6 fresh strawberries, hulled and quartered
1 kiwi, peeled and cut into 6 rounds
6 fresh mint sprigs for garnish (optional)

Cut off both ends of the oranges down to the flesh. Turn one of the cut ends towards you and use a sharp, slender knife to cut off the rind down to the flesh in a spiral; the fruit will fall out in a barrel shape. Cut each orange into 5 equal crosswise slices. Place a hollowed-out orange rind, cut side up, on each of 6 plates and fan 5 orange slices over the top of the rind. Arrange the strawberries and kiwi slices on top of the orange slices, and garnish each serving with a mint sprig, if desired.   *Makes 6 servings*

OATMEAL WITH FRESH FRUIT AND CURRANTS

Comfort food at its best.

2 cups (6 oz / 185 g) old-fashioned rolled oats
6 cups (48 fl oz / 1.5 l) water
3 tablespoons packed brown sugar
¼ teaspoon ground nutmeg
½ teaspoon ground cinnamon
¼ teaspoon salt
3 tablespoons dried currants
1 banana, peeled, halved lengthwise, and chopped
1 ½ oz (45 g) dried apricots, chopped (¼ cup)

In a large, heavy saucepan, combine all the ingredients and bring to a boil. Reduce heat to a simmer and cook, stirring occasionally, for 5 minutes. Serve with milk.   *Makes 6 servings*

CINNAMON-RASPBERRY MUFFINS

The addition of sour cream gives these fruit-flavored muffins extra moistness.

1¾ cups (7 oz/220 g) all-purpose flour
1½ teaspoons baking powder
1 cup (8 oz/250 g) sugar
1 teaspoon ground cinnamon
1 cup (8 oz/250 g) sour cream
4 tablespoons (2 oz/60 g) unsalted butter, melted
2 teaspoons grated lemon zest
1 egg, lightly beaten
⅓ cup mashed fresh strawberries
1 cup (4 oz/125 g) fresh raspberries

❧ Preheat the oven to 350°F (180°C). Lightly butter 12 muffin cups.

❧ In a medium bowl, combine the flour, baking powder, sugar, and cinnamon and stir well. In a large bowl, combine all the remaining ingredients except the raspberries. Stir well.

❧ Add the flour mixture to the sour cream mixture and stir just until combined; the batter should be slightly lumpy. Gently fold in the raspberries and spoon the batter into the prepared muffin cups. Bake for 35 to 40 minutes, or until a skewer inserted in the center of a muffin comes out clean. Serve warm.   *Makes 12 muffins*

QUINCE WITH STAR ANISE

If quinces are unavailable, gently simmer pears for 20 minutes and let cool in the syrup.

4 quinces, peeled, halved, and cored
1 cup (8 fl oz/250 ml) dry white wine
½ cup (4 oz/125 g) sugar
8 star anise
1 vanilla bean, split lengthwise
1 kaffir lime leaf* or strip of lime zest

Put the quinces in a large saucepan and add water to cover. Stir in all the remaining ingredients. Bring to a boil, reduce heat to a simmer, cover, and cook for 2 hours, or until the quinces are soft and pink.

Using a slotted spoon, transfer the quinces to shallow bowls. Increase heat to high and boil the poaching liquid until reduced by half. Spoon some of the liquid over each serving and garnish with a star anise.   *Makes 6 to 8 servings*

*Kaffir lime leaves have an intriguing citrus scent and are available in specialty produce stores or Asian markets.

The Harbor House Inn

Elk, California

uilt in 1916, the Harbor House is a Craftsman-style redwood gem that sits high on a cliff overlooking Greenwood Cove, with its pounding Pacific surf and spectacular rock formations. Just seventeen miles south of the town of Mendocino, the house is an enlarged replica of the showcase Redwood Home displayed at the 1915 Pan-Pacific Exhibition in San Francisco. It was built for the manager of the Goodyear Lumber Company, whose mill was on the beach just below the house. Today the peaceful inn is warm and welcoming, perfect for long relaxing stays. Guests enjoy four-course dinners and gourmet breakfasts and stay in the charming guest rooms and private 1930s-era cottages.

Since Sam and Elle Haynes purchased Harbor House in 1998, they have lavished considerable attention on the inn's decor and cuisine, expanded the wine list, and created an English-style coastal garden behind the house. Guests socialize or contemplate life while relaxing in Adirondack chairs facing the sea, admire the flower beds and organic garden, and take the steps leading down to a private rocky beach. Just a short drive away are the acclaimed wineries and tasting rooms of Anderson Valley, art galleries and shops in Mendocino, and hiking trails among ancient redwood forests in Samuel P. Taylor state park.

At the end of the day, welcoming log fires make Harbor Houses's stately redwood-paneled sitting room a perfect place for guests to assemble before dinner. The intimate dining room, with its spectacular ocean views, cozy fireplace, crisp white linens, and soft music, is a wonderful setting for chef Paul Ciardiello's menu of California cuisine inspired by the flavors of Tuscany and Provence. Ciardiello's menus change every evening to feature seafood from nearby coastal waters, the finest meats and poultry, and local garden-fresh produce. Harbor House hosts a popular series of winemaker dinners, with informal receptions that present a noted vintner and a food and wine pairing discussion by chef Ciardiello. Afterwards a dinner created by the talented chef brings out the best in the selected wines. The following recipes were created for Menus and Music by chef Paul Ciardiello.

Menu

Minestra

NAVARRO CHARDONNAY

❧

Grilled New York Strip Steaks
with Cherry Sauce, Roast Potatoes, and Succotash

GROTH CABERNET

❧

Warm Spinach, Crab, and Potato Salad

GREENWOOD RIDGE WHITE RIESLING

❧

Tiramisù

ESSENCIA ORANGE MUSCAT

BRIAN LAMPRELL

Wine makes daily living easier, less hurried,
with fewer tensions and more tolerance.

—BENJAMIN FRANKLIN

🍇 MINESTRA 🍇

A hearty soup for a blustery day.

1 tablespoon olive oil
1 pound (500 g) country pork ribs
1 onion, diced
¼ cup (2 fl oz/60 ml) dry sherry
¾ cup (5 oz/155 g) dried cannellini beans, soaked in water to cover
   overnight, rinsed, and drained
8 cups (64 fl oz/2 l) chicken stock (see Basics) or canned low-salt chicken
   broth
1 tablespoon minced fresh thyme
1 head escarole or chard, cored and chopped crosswise into ribbons
Salt and freshly ground pepper to taste
Grated Parmesan cheese for sprinkling

🌱 In a large Dutch oven or a heatproof casserole, heat the olive oil over high heat until almost smoking. Brown the pork ribs in batches on all sides. Transfer the ribs to a plate. Reduce heat to medium and sauté the onion until translucent, about 3 minutes. Add the sherry and stir to scrape up any browned bits on the bottom of the pan. Add the beans, stock or broth, ribs, and thyme. Increase heat to high and bring to a boil. Reduce heat to low, cover, and simmer until the ribs are tender, about 1½ hours.

🌱 Using a slotted spoon, transfer the ribs to a plate. Pick the meat off the bones and add it to the soup. Bring the soup to a boil and stir in the escarole or chard, salt, and pepper. Cook until the escarole or chard wilts. Ladle the soup into shallow bowls and sprinkle with Parmesan cheese. *Makes 6 servings*

GRILLED NEW YORK STRIP STEAKS WITH CHERRY SAUCE, ROAST POTATOES, AND SUCCOTASH

Complementary and contrasting flavors balance perfectly in this outstanding dish. Fava beans replace limas in Chef Ciardiello's variation on traditional succotash.

1 cup (8 fl oz/250 ml) dry red wine
1 cup (8 fl oz/250 ml) olive oil
⅓ cup (3 oz/90 g) Dijon mustard
2 garlic cloves, minced
4 New York strip steaks

CHERRY SAUCE
2 cups (16 fl oz/500 ml) veal stock (see Basics) or canned low-salt beef broth
¾ cup (4 oz/125 g) dried cherries*
1 teaspoon minced fresh tarragon

ROAST POTATOES
12 small red potatoes, halved
2 tablespoons olive oil
Salt and freshly ground pepper to taste

SUCCOTASH
24 fava beans, shelled
4 tablespoons (2 oz/60 g) unsalted butter
Kernels cut from 4 ears of corn
1 red bell pepper, seeded, deribbed, and chopped

☙ In a baking dish, combine the wine, olive oil, mustard, and garlic. Add the steaks and turn to coat. Cover and refrigerate, turning occasionally, for 36 hours.

☙ To make the sauce: In a medium saucepan, boil the stock or broth until reduced by one-third. Reduce heat to medium-low, add the dried cherries and tarragon, and simmer until the cherries are soft, about 5 minutes. Set aside and keep warm.

☙ To make the roast potatoes: Preheat the oven to 400°F (200°C). Arrange the potatoes in a single layer in a baking dish, toss with the olive oil to coat, and sprinkle with salt and pepper. Bake for 35 minutes, or until tender. Set aside and keep warm.

🍂 While the potatoes are cooking, remove the steak from the refrigerator, prepare a fire in an outdoor grill or preheat the broiler, and make the succotash: Blanch the fava beans in salted boiling water for 1 minute. Drain and rinse under cold water. Pinch open the end of each bean and pop it from its skin.

🍂 In a large frying pan, melt the butter over medium heat and sauté the corn, fava beans, and bell pepper for 10 minutes, or until tender. Set aside and keep warm.

🍂 Drain the steaks and grill or broil them for 5 to 7 minutes on each side for medium rare. Transfer to a plate and let rest for 3 minutes.

🍂 To serve, place a mound of succotash in the center of each of 4 warmed plates. Top with a steak and arrange the roasted potatoes around the succotash. Spoon some cherry sauce over and serve immediately.   *Makes 4 servings*

*Dried cherries are available at specialty foods stores or by mail from Cherry Republic (see Resources).

Warm Spinach, Crab, and Potato Salad

Serve as a first course, or as a delicious main-dish salad with crusty bread.

4 Yukon Gold potatoes, peeled and diced
2 tablespoons unsalted butter
2 bunches spinach, stemmed
Salt and freshly ground pepper to taste
8 ounces (250 g) fresh lump crabmeat, picked over for shell
Champagne Vinaigrette (recipe follows)

Cook the potatoes in salted boiling water for 5 minutes, or until tender.
Drain and let cool.

In a large frying pan, melt the butter over medium-high heat. Add the
spinach, salt, and pepper and sauté until the spinach wilts, about 3 minutes.

In a large bowl, combine the crab, spinach, and potatoes. Toss with the
vinaigrette and serve immediately.   *Makes 4 to 6 servings*

Champagne Vinaigrette

2 tablespoons Champagne vinegar
7 tablespoons (3½ fl oz/105 ml) olive oil or walnut oil
1½ tablespoons Dijon mustard
1 teaspoon minced fresh thyme
1 tablespoon minced shallot
Salt and freshly ground pepper to taste

In a medium bowl, whisk all the ingredients together.
                    Makes about ¾ cup (6 fl oz/180 ml)

TIRAMISÙ

Chef Paul Ciardiello's version of this luscious Italian dessert is made as individual servings.

¾ cup (6 fl oz/ 180 ml) cold brewed espresso
¾ cup (6 fl oz/ 180 ml) sweet Marsala wine
24 ladyfingers
4 egg yolks
⅓ cup (3 oz/ 90 g) sugar
4 egg whites
2 cups (16 oz/ 500 g) mascarpone cheese* at room temperature
2 tablespoons vanilla extract
Unsweetened cocoa powder for dusting

In a pie plate, combine the espresso and Marsala. Briefly dunk each lady-finger into the mixture. Quickly stack 4 ladyfingers "Lincoln Log" fashion to make a square on each of 6 plates.

In a medium bowl, beat the egg yolks and sugar until a slowly dissolving ribbon forms on the surface when the beater is lifted. In a large bowl, beat the egg whites until stiff, glossy peaks form.

In a large bowl, beat the mascarpone and vanilla until smooth. Stir in the yolk mixture until well blended. Fold in the whites.

Ladle ¾ cup (6 oz/ 185 g) of the mascarpone mixture into the center of each square of ladyfingers and refrigerate for at least 4 hours or overnight before serving. Dust with cocoa powder and serve.   *Makes 6 servings*

* Mascarpone, a delicately flavored triple-cream cheese from Lombardy, is available in many grocery stores and most specialty foods stores.

The Harbor House Inn

The Ink House

St. Helena, California

Built in 1884 by Theron H. Ink for his family, this grand old country house offers comfort and Victorian elegance in the middle of beautiful Napa Valley. The building's Italianate-Victorian architecture has earned it a listing on the National Register of Historic Places. The inn is owned and personally managed by Diane De Filipi, a welcoming innkeeper who oversees every detail.

Guests enjoy socializing and reading in the two delightful first-floor parlors of the house, complete with concert grand piano, fireplace, pump organ, crystal chandeliers, and original stained glass windows. The charming second-story guest bedrooms have stunning views and are individually decorated with antiques and the innkeeper's family heirlooms. At the very top of the house is the Ink House's distinctive glass-enclosed observatory. Fifty feet above the valley floor, guests have 360 degree panoramic views of Napa's well-tended vineyards and forested hillsides, the sunset, or hot air balloons floating by in the early morning air. A picnic table and swing await in the garden, and there is a cozy games room for a game of pool or darts in the stone-walled basement. Bicycles are available for quiet rides down vineyard-lined Whitehall Lane, and the museums and shops of St. Helena as well as many of Napa's best known wineries and restaurants are just minutes away. In the late afternoon, wine and appetizers are served in the Ink House living room and local winemakers are often invited to pour their selections and share their winemaking secrets.

Each morning a bountiful breakfast, including fruits, egg dishes, freshly baked breads and muffins, and often the innkeeper's signature "Bella Torta," is served at the inn's elegant dining room table. Diane De Filipi created the following recipes.

. . . where the soil is sublimated under the sun and stars to something finer, and the wine is bottled poetry . . .

—Robert Louis Stevenson

Breakfast Menu

Carrot Bread

❧

Seasonal Fresh Fruit

❧

Bella Torta

Wine-Tasting Appetizer Menu

White Bean and Pesto Spread

❧

Thai Peanut Dipping Sauce

❧

Sun-Dried Tomato Spread

❧

Maui Wowie Chutney

 Carrot Bread

*This moist, fragrant sweet bread served with seasonal fresh fruit
is a delicious way to start the day.*

1 ½ cups (7 ½ oz / 235 g) all-purpose flour
1 teaspoon baking powder
½ teaspoon baking soda
1 teaspoon ground cinnamon
¼ teaspoon ground nutmeg
¼ teaspoon ground ginger
½ teaspoon salt
2 eggs
1 cup (7 oz / 220 g) packed brown sugar
⅓ cup (3 fl oz / 80 ml) canola oil
2 tablespoons maple syrup
1 ¼ cups (6 oz / 185 g) packed grated carrots (about 2 peeled carrots)
½ cup (4 oz / 125 g) canned crushed pineapple, drained
¼ cup (1 ½ oz / 45 g) raisins
¼ cup (1 oz / 30 g) shredded coconut (optional)

Preheat the oven to 350°F (180°C). Butter the bottom and sides of a
9-by-5-inch (23-by-13-cm) loaf pan.

In a medium bowl, combine the flour, baking powder, baking soda,
cinnamon, nutmeg, ginger, and salt. Stir well.

In a small bowl, whisk the eggs until foamy. Stir in the brown sugar, oil,
and maple syrup. Add the egg mixture to the flour mixture and mix well. Stir
in the carrots, pineapple, raisins, and coconut, if using. Pour the batter into
the prepared pan and bake for 1 hour, or until a skewer inserted in the center
comes out clean. Cut into slices to serve.

Makes one 9-by-5-inch (23-by-13-cm) loaf

BELLA TORTA

Chef innkeeper Diane DeFilipi's signature breakfast dish.

3 bunches fresh spinach, stemmed and rinsed, or one 10-ounce package
   thawed frozen chopped spinach
5 eggs
¼ cup (1 oz/30 g) dried bread crumbs
¼ teaspoon ground nutmeg
¼ cup (2 fl oz/60 ml) heavy cream or half and half
1 tablespoon pine nuts
¼ cup (2 fl oz/60 ml) milk
1 teaspoon dried Italian herbs, crumbled
Salt and freshly ground pepper to taste
1 tablespoon unsalted butter
4 oil-packed sun-dried tomatoes, drained and chopped
4 marinated artichoke hearts, drained
4 large, thin slices provolone cheese

➥ Preheat the oven to 350°F (180°C). Butter an 8-inch square (20-cm)
baking dish.
➥ If using fresh spinach, put it in a large saucepan, cover, and cook over
medium-high heat until it wilts. Set aside to cool. Squeeze the moisture from
the cooked fresh or the thawed spinach.
➥ In a medium bowl, lightly beat 1 of the eggs. Add the spinach, bread
crumbs, nutmeg, cream, and pine nuts. Stir until well blended.
➥ In a medium bowl, lightly beat the remaining 4 eggs, milk, herbs, salt,
and pepper. In a large frying pan, melt the butter over low heat, add the
eggs, and stir for 2 or 3 minutes, or until barely set. Immediately remove
from heat and spread the eggs evenly in the bottom of the prepared dish.
Arrange the tomatoes evenly over the eggs. Top with the provolone. Top
with the spinach mixture, sprinkle with pepper, and arrange the artichoke
hearts evenly on top.
➥ Bake for 30 minutes. Let cool for 5 minutes. Cut into squares and serve.

Makes 4 servings

Wine-Tasting Appetizers

Serve any of the following dips and/or spreads with a selection of red and white wines for a wine-tasting, or with a glass of wine before dinner. When serving a large party, you can easily double or triple the recipes.

White Bean and Pesto Spread

Serve this as a dip for crudités, such as baby carrots, radishes, broccoli and cauliflower florets, and cherry tomatoes, or as a spread for crackers or crostini (see Basics).

⅓ cup (3 oz/90 g) mayonnaise
One 15-oz (425 g) can cannellini beans, drained and rinsed
1½ tablespoons fresh lemon juice
¼ teaspoon salt
2 tablespoons pesto

In a blender or food processor, combine all the ingredients and process until smooth, about 1 minute. Transfer to a bowl, cover, and refrigerate for 2 hours to chill. *Makes about 1½ cups (12 oz/360g)*

Thai Peanut Dipping Sauce

Serve as a dip with raw vegetables or with cocktail-sized skewers of beef and chicken.

¼ cup (2 oz/60 g) packed brown sugar
1 tablespoon soy sauce
1 tablespoon rice vinegar
¼ cup (2 oz/60 g) creamy peanut butter
1 teaspoon Asian sesame oil
½ teaspoon chili oil
½ teaspoon grated fresh ginger
1 tablespoon water

In a small pan, combine the sugar, soy sauce, and vinegar and cook over low heat for 3 to 4 minutes, or until the sugar dissolves. Stir in all the remaining ingredients and cook for 3 minutes. Remove from heat. Serve warm or at room temperature, or cover and refrigerate for up to 2 days; rewarm over low heat to serve. *Makes about ¾ cup (6 fl oz/375 ml)*

Sun-Dried Tomato Spread

Serve with crackers or crostini (see Basics), or as a dip for crudités.

10 ounces (315 g) natural cream cheese at room temperature
12 oil-packed sun-dried tomatoes, drained (reserve oil) and chopped
1½ tablespoons reserved sun-dried tomato oil
6 garlic cloves, chopped
2 tablespoons milk
1 tablespoon chopped fresh basil

In a blender or food processor, combine all the ingredients and process until smooth. Transfer to a bowl, cover, and refrigerate for at least 2 hours or up to 2 days. *Makes about 2 cups (8 oz / 250 g)*

Maui Wowie Chutney

Serve over cream cheese or baked Brie or alone with crackers. If Maui onions are unavailable, use Walla Wallas, Texas Sweets, or Vidalias.

2 tablespoons olive oil
1 Maui onion, finely diced
1 red onion, finely diced
1 tart apple, such as Fuji, Gala, or Granny Smith, peeled, cored,
  and finely diced
1 garlic clove, minced
2 tablespoon golden raisins
½ tablespoon Worcestershire sauce
Salt and freshly ground pepper to taste

In a large frying pan, heat the olive oil over medium heat and sauté the onions for 5 minutes, or until golden. Reduce heat to low, add the apple, and sauté for 10 minutes. Stir in all the remaining ingredients and cook for 5 minutes. Let cool, cover, and refrigerate for at least 2 hours or up to 2 days.

Makes about 2 cups (8 oz / 250 g)

Inn on the Twenty

Jordan, Ontario

Located in the heart of Niagara's award-winning wine region, Inn on the Twenty guests have a chance to relax and enjoy luxurious accommodations and the best in regional food and wine. Helen Young and Len Pennachetti have transformed a former 1871 warehouse into a stylish, internationally-acclaimed restaurant, and in 1996 they established a comfortably elegant inn that blends original art, antiques, and contemporary furnishings. Just next door is Cave Spring Cellars, founded in 1986 by grape grower Leonard Pennachetti and winemaker Angelo Pavan and one of Canada's finest wineries.

Inn on the Twenty guests stay in elegant, restful suites, each complete with a stone fireplace and whirlpool bath. Breakfast is a leisurely affair that includes an array of freshly baked pastries and breads, seasonal fruits, quiche, yogurt, housemade granola and a choice of omelettes, frittatas, and brioche French toast. Thus fortified, guests enjoy visits to nearby Niagara Falls and picturesque Niagara-on-the-Lake with its many shops and the acclaimed Shaw Festival, one of North America's finest summer theater festivals. The tiny village of Jordan, with its tree-lined main street located beside Twenty Mile Creek, offers shopping and antique hunting, and there is a small museum devoted to its early settlers and an authentically restored pioneer settlement. Guests also take tours and taste fine Niagara wines at Cave Spring Cellars. The combination of the sheltering effect of the Niagara Escarpment and the moderating influence of Lake Ontario give this region a micro-climate favorable for growing classic varieties of the world's great cool-climate wine grapes.

On the Twenty, Ontario's first and best-known estate winery restaurant, is consistently rated as one of the finest restaurants in Canada. Dedicated to regional cuisine, chef Rob Fracchioni makes the most of local peaches, apples, pears, berries, quail, trout, and organically-grown vegetables, herbs, and greens. The restaurant has a secure relationship with local producers, and unique and surprising products find their way to the kitchen door throughout the seasons. Chef Fracchioni's exciting dishes complement the unique character of Niagara's finest wines. The restaurant's wine list is exclusively VQA Niagara and represents the best vintages of the region. The following dinner was created by Rob Fracchioni and the Harvest Peach Tart by pastry chef Anna Olson.

VINELAND ESTATES WINERY
1999
DRY RIESLING
750ml • NIAGARA PENINSULA • VQA 10.7%alc./vol.
Product of Canada • White Wine • Vin Blanc • Produit du Canada

CAVE SPRING
Indian Summer
1999
RIESLING
VQA NIAGARA PENINSULA VQA
Select Late Harvest
CAVE SPRING CELLARS, JORDAN, ONTARIO, CANADA
WHITE WINE/PRODUCT OF CANADA • VIN BLANC/PRODUIT DU CANADA
12.5% alc./vol. 375 mL

THIRTY BENCH
White Wine / Vin Blanc
1998
SEMI DRY RIESLING DEMI SEC
VQA - NIAGARA PENINSULA - VQA
THIRTY BENCH VINEYARD SELECT
Estate Bottled
THIRTY BENCH WINES
Beamsville, Ontario
PRODUCT OF CANADA - PRODUIT DU CANADA
11.5%alc./vol. 750ml

PILLITTERI ESTATES Winery
1999
VIDAL ICEWINE
VQA Niagara Peninsula VQA
SWEET WHITE WINE
VIN BLANC DOUX
VQA
10.0% alc./vol.
200 ml
PRODUCT OF CANADA

Inniskillin

OKANAGAN
1997
MERITAGE
VQA OKANAGAN VALLEY VQA
750 ml DRY RED WINE / VIN ROUGE SEC 12.0% alc./vol.

KONZELMANN ESTATE WINERY
FAMILY OWNED SINCE 1893
1998
VQA NIAGARA PENINSULA VQA
PINOT NOIR (0)
(Spaetburgunder)
Dry Red Wine / Vin Rouge sec
12.0 % alc./vol. 750 ml
NIAGARA-ON-THE-LAKE, ONTARIO
Product of Canada Produit du Canada

HILLEBRAND ESTATES
Glenlake Vineyard
1999
VQA • NIAGARA PENINSULA • VQA
CHARDONNAY
BARREL FERMENTED
BARREL 7013
JUPILLE FOREST OAK
WHITE WINE/VIN BLANC
750mL 13.9%alc./vol.
PRODUCT OF CANADA/PRODUIT DU CANADA
VINTED BY HILLEBRAND ESTATES, NIAGARA-ON-THE-LAKE, ONTARIO

Château des Charmes
PAUL BOSC ESTATE VINEYARD
CHARDONNAY
VQA • NIAGARA PENINSULA • VQA
13% alc./vol. 750 ml
WHITE WINE VIN BLANC
CHÂTEAU DES CHARMES WINES LTD., NIAGARA-ON-THE-LAKE, ONTARIO
PRODUCT OF CANADA - PRODUIT DU CANADA

CAVE SPRING
1999
Reserve Réserve
RIESLING
VQA NIAGARA PENINSULA VQA
ESTATE BOTTLED
CAVE SPRING CELLARS, JORDAN, ONTARIO, CANADA
WHITE WINE/PRODUCT OF CANADA • VIN BLANC/PRODUIT DU CANADA
13.0%alc./vol. 750 mL

Stoney Ridge
750 mL 1999 12.0% alc./vol.
Reserve
Riesling
VQA NIAGARA PENINSULA VQA
STONEY RIDGE CELLARS, VINELAND, ONTARIO
WHITE WINE - VIN BLANC
PRODUCT OF CANADA/PRODUIT DU CANADA

THE COLLECTORS' CHOICE
CHARDONNAY
VQA - NIAGARA PENINSULA - VQA
Barrel Aged
1998
VQA
HILLEBRAND ESTATES
PRODUCED AND BOTTLED BY
HILLEBRAND ESTATES, NIAGARA-ON-THE-LAKE, ONTARIO, CANADA
WHITE WINE • PRODUCT OF CANADA VIN BLANC • PRODUIT DU CANADA
12.5% alc./vol. 750 mL

HENRY of PELHAM
FAMILY ESTATE
1999
RESERVE
Chardonnay
VQA NIAGARA PENINSULA VQA
750 mL WHITE WINE • VIN BLANC 13.0% alc./vol.
PRODUCT OF CANADA PRODUIT DU CANADA

PELEE ISLAND WINERY
1999
Merlot
12.2% alc./vol. 750 ml
RED WINE/VIN ROUGE
CELLARED BY PELEE ISLAND WINERY, KINGSVILLE, ONTARIO, CANADA,
FROM IMPORTED AND DOMESTIC WINES

Menu

Salad of Arugula, Roasted Pears, Beets,
and Herbed Goat Cheese

CAVE SPRING CELLARS RIESLING RESERVE OR CHARDONNAY BENCH

❧

Roast Cornish Hens Stuffed
with Sourdough, Roasted Peppers, and Sausage

CAVE SPRING CELLARS GAMAY RESERVE

❧

Cheddar Cheese with Thyme-Infused Honey

CAVE SPRING CELLARS OFF DRY RIESLING

❧

Harvest Peach Tart

CAVE SPRING CELLARS INDIAN SUMMER RIESLING

Salad of Arugula, Roasted Pears, Beets, and Herbed Goat Cheese

A superb salad of perfectly balanced tastes, colors, and textures.

2 Bartlett pears, peeled, cored, and cut into eighths
¾ cup (6 fl oz / 180 ml) brandy
4 tablespoons (2 oz / 60 g) unsalted butter, diced
¼ cup (2 oz / 60 g) sugar
Salt and freshly ground pepper to taste
2 red bell peppers, roasted and peeled (see Basics)
4 tablespoons (2 fl oz / 60 ml) extra-virgin olive oil, plus more for coating
2 beets, stems trimmed to ½ inch (12 mm)
½ cup (4 fl oz / 125 ml) red wine vinegar
½ orange, quartered
1 lemon, quartered
1 log (5 oz / 155 g) fresh white goat cheese
1 tablespoon minced fresh thyme
1 tablespoon minced fresh chives
1 tablespoon minced fresh basil
2 bunches arugula, stemmed
2 teaspoons balsamic vinegar

Preheat the oven to 350°F (180°C). Arrange the pear slices in an 8-inch (20-cm) square baking dish. Pour in the brandy, dot the pears with butter, and sprinkle with the sugar, salt, and pepper. Bake for 15 minutes, tossing the pears every 5 minutes. Remove from the oven and let cool to room temperature.

Cut the peppers into thin strips. In a small bowl, combine the peppers, 2 tablespoons of the olive oil, and salt and pepper to taste. Toss to coat. Set aside.

In a large pot, combine the beets, vinegar, orange, and lemon. Add water to cover and bring to a boil. Cook for 15 to 20 minutes, or until tender. Drain and set aside to cool to room temperature. Trim, peel, and cut the beets into thin wedges.

(continued on following page)

Preheat the oven to 350°F (180°C). Line a baking sheet with parchment paper. Cut the goat cheese into thin rounds. In a medium bowl, combine the herbs. Coat the goat cheese rounds with the herbs and transfer to the prepared pan. Bake for 3 minutes, or until soft to the touch.

In a medium bowl, toss the arugula with the remaining 2 tablespoons olive oil and the balsamic vinegar. Place a small mound of arugula in the center of each of 4 plates and arrange the pears, beets, and peppers around it. Using a spatula, transfer a round of goat cheese to the top of each mound of arugula and serve.

Makes 4 servings

STEPHEN DOMINICK

Wine rejoices the heart of man and joy is the mother of all virtues.

—JOHANN WOLFGANG VON GOETHE

Roast Cornish Hens Stuffed with Sourdough, Roasted Peppers, and Sausage

3 tablespoons unsalted butter

1 small onion, finely chopped

1 small carrot, peeled and finely chopped

1 celery stalk, finely chopped

1 shallot, minced

8 ounces (250 g) sausage, finely chopped

1 red bell pepper, roasted, peeled, and cut into thin strips (see Basics)

1 tablespoon minced garlic

1½ tablespoons minced fresh thyme

½ teaspoon minced fresh rosemary

Salt and freshly ground pepper to taste

½ day-old loaf sourdough bread, cut into ¼-inch (6-mm) dice, about
    4 cups (8 oz/250 g)

1 cup (8 fl oz/250 ml) chicken stock (see Basics) or canned low-salt chicken
    broth, heated

4 Cornish hens

2 tablespoons olive oil

In a large frying pan, melt 1 tablespoon of the butter over medium-low heat and sauté the onion, carrot, celery, shallot, and sausage for 7 minutes. Add the roasted pepper, garlic, thyme, rosemary, salt, and pepper and sauté for 5 minutes. Stir in the bread cubes and add stock or broth until the bread is slightly moistened. Remove from heat and let cool.

Preheat the oven to 350°F (180°C). Line a large baking dish with parchment paper.

Rinse the hens well and pat them dry. Stuff the bread mixture into each hen cavity and transfer the hens to the prepared dish. Rub the hens with olive oil. Cut up the remaining 2 tablespoons butter and add it to the bottom of the pan. Bake the hens, basting occasionally, for 50 minutes, or until the juices run clear when a thigh is pierced. Arrange a hen in the center of each of 4 plates and serve immediately. *Makes 4 servings*

CHEDDAR WITH THYME-INFUSED HONEY

On the Twenty serves five-year-old Balderson Cheddar, but any fine, aged sharp Cheddar cheese may be used. The honey softens the sharpness of the cheese without masking its flavor.

1 cup (12 oz / 375 g) honey
1 bunch thyme
12 ounces (375 g) aged sharp Cheddar cheese, cut into 4 pieces, at room
  temperature
4 thyme flowers for garnish (optional)

In a small saucepan, combine the honey and thyme. Slowly bring to a boil over low heat, stirring occasionally. Simmer for 2 minutes, then remove from heat. Let stand for 15 minutes. Remove the thyme sprigs; if a few leaves fall off, leave them in the honey.

Place 1 piece of cheese on each of 4 plates. Drizzle with honey and garnish with a thyme flower, if you like. *Makes 4 servings*

HARVEST PEACH TART

Based on the classic French tarte Tatin, which is traditionally prepared with apples, this tart captures the fabulous flavor of fresh summer peaches. Choose firm peaches that will hold their shape during cooking.

14 ounces (440 g) thawed frozen puff pastry
4 tablespoons (2 oz/60 g) unsalted butter
½ cup (3½ oz/105 g) packed brown sugar
½ teaspoon ground cinnamon
1 tablespoon brandy or rum
6 peaches, peeled, pitted, and quartered (see Basics)

Preheat the oven to 375°F (190°C). On a lightly floured surface, roll the puff pastry out to a 10-inch (25-cm) circle about ¼ inch (6 mm) thick. Transfer to a small jelly roll pan lined with parchment paper and refrigerate for 30 minutes.

In a small frying pan, melt the butter over medium heat. Stir in the brown sugar and cinnamon and cook until blended and bubbling. Carefully stir in the brandy or rum (it may ignite as the alcohol burns off). Pour the mixture into the bottom of a 10-inch (25-cm) pie plate.

Overlap the peach slices in concentric circles over the sugar mixture. Lay the puff pastry over the peaches, tucking the edges of the dough down into the dish around the peaches. With a sharp knife, cut steam vents.

Bake for 25 to 30 minutes, or until the pastry is golden brown. Remove from the oven and let cool.

Place a plate over the pie plate and invert to unmold the tart, giving the bottom a firm whack to release the peaches at the bottom. Cut into wedges to serve.

Makes one 10-inch (25-cm) tart

The Kenwood Inn & Spa

Kenwood, California

Combining the intimate charms of a bed and breakfast with exceptional standards of luxury, Terry and Roseann Grimm have created an enchanting, Tuscan-inspired retreat that overlooks acres of rolling estate vineyards in the heart of Sonoma Valley. Kenwood's five, vine-covered buildings cluster around an inviting swimming pool and a romantic courtyard garden with fountains, herbs, roses, and persimmon, fig, and olive trees. Spa rooms open up off the courtyard, and from under shady grape arbors guests easily imagine they are enjoying the peaceful atmosphere of a sumptuous Italian country villa.

Each of Kenwood's twelve suites has a balcony or private terrace, and Roseann Grimm has decorated their interiors with French and Italian antiques, luxurious fabrics, and warm terra cotta-colored walls that give a flattering rosy glow. Fresh cookies, flowers, and a welcoming bottle of wine await in front of the fireplace.

Guests spend their time visiting acclaimed wineries just up the street or the village of Glen Ellen, which was once home to renowned food writer M.F.K. Fisher. Just west of Glen Ellen is Jack London State Historic Park, a museum and more than 800 acres of vineyards, orchards, and redwoods dedicated to the literary legend, who immortalized this region as "The Valley of the Moon" in his 1913 novel by that name. Guests also enjoy sightseeing, shopping, and dining in the historic town of Sonoma, while others find that after a day of swimming, reading, and basking in the sun, the universe has shrunk to the size of Kenwood's delightful inner courtyard. The inn's excellent small spa offers services such as therapeutic massage and innovative skincare and body treatments for overnight guests, as well as day use for those who stop in to visit.

Each morning a gourmet breakfast is served on an outdoor dining terrace in the garden or in the comfortable main house. The Mediterranean-inspired breakfasts are served in courses and highlight the fresh flavors of Sonoma garden vegetables, fruits, and herbs.

KAY CARLSON

Drink wine, this is life eternal,
This, all that youth will give you:
It is the season for wine, roses, and friends
drinking together,
Be happy for this moment—it is all life is.

—OMAR KHAYYAM

Breakfast Menu

Berries and Plums
with Sangría Reduction

❧

Braised Saffron Potatoes
with Poached Eggs, Smoked Salmon,
and Grilled Asparagus

Berries and Plums with Sangría Reduction

½ bottle (12 fl oz/375 ml) dry red table wine

1 cup (8 oz/250 g) plus 4 tablespoons (2 oz/60 g) sugar

1 orange

3 lemons

1½ cups (6 oz/375 g) fresh strawberries, hulled and quartered

2 large black plums, halved and pitted

1½ cups (6 oz/375 g) fresh raspberries

1½ cups (6 oz/375 g) fresh blackberries

4 mint sprigs

In a large saucepan, combine the wine and 1 cup (8 oz/250 g) of the sugar. Bring to a boil, stirring to dissolve the sugar. Using a potato peeler, cut the zest from the lemons and orange. Juice the fruit. Add the zest to the wine mixture and pour in orange juice and all but 2 tablespoons of the lemon juice. Simmer until reduced by half. Remove from heat and let cool; strain and set aside.

In a medium bowl, combine the strawberries, 1 tablespoon of the remaining lemon juice, and 2 tablespoons of the sugar. Stir gently until the sugar dissolves; set aside.

Cut each plum half into 4 wedges. In a medium bowl, combine the plums, the remaining 1 tablespoon lemon juice, and the remaining 2 tablespoons sugar.

In a medium bowl, combine the raspberries, blackberries, and one-third of the sangría reduction.

To serve, divide the strawberries equally among 4 dessert plates. Top with the plums, raspberries, and blackberries. Spoon sangría reduction over the fruit to make a pool on each plate and garnish with a mint sprig.

Makes 4 servings

BRAISED SAFFRON POTATOES WITH POACHED EGGS, SMOKED SALMON, AND ASPARAGUS

2 large russet potatoes, peeled and halved lengthwise
2 cups (16 fl oz / 500 ml) chicken stock (see Basics) or canned low-salt
   chicken broth
2 cups (16 fl oz / 500 ml) water
2 tablespoons cold unsalted butter, cut into bits
6 saffron threads
1 teaspoon salt, plus salt to taste
12 asparagus spears
1 tablespoon olive oil
Freshly ground pepper to taste
1 tablespoon cider vinegar
4 eggs
6 oz (185 g) thinly sliced smoked salmon
Lemon-Spinach Cream Sauce (recipe follows)

Preheat the oven to 425°F (220°C). Cut off the ends of the potatoes. Arrange the potatoes in a single layer in an 8-inch (20-cm) square baking dish and cover with the stock or broth and water. Sprinkle in the butter, saffron, and the 1 teaspoon salt. Bake for 1½ hours, or until tender. Drain and keep warm.

In a covered steamer over boiling water, steam the asparagus until crisp-tender, 3 to 6 minutes depending on thickness. Transfer to a bowl and toss with the olive oil, salt, and pepper.

Meanwhile, in a large frying pan, bring 1½ inches (4 cm) water to a boil. Add the vinegar and reduce heat to a simmer. Add the eggs one at a time and poach for 3 or 4 minutes. Using a slotted spoon, transfer to a plate.

Place 1 potato half on each of 4 plates and drape a generous slice of smoked salmon over one end. Place a poached egg on top and lay 3 asparagus spears to the side of each potato. Spoon the sauce over the eggs and serve immediately.   *Makes 4 servings*

LEMON-SPINACH CREAM SAUCE

1 cup (8 fl oz/250 ml) heavy cream
Grated zest of 2 lemons
4 tablespoons (2 oz/60 g) unsalted butter
½ cup (1 oz/30 g) chopped fresh spinach
Salt and freshly ground pepper to taste

In a medium saucepan, bring the cream to a simmer and cook until reduced by half. Reduce heat to low, stir in the lemon zest and butter, and cook for 10 minutes. Stir in the spinach, salt, and pepper. Use now, or let cool, cover, and refrigerate for up to 3 days; reheat over low heat.

Makes about ½ cup (4 oz/125 ml)

Madrona Manor
Wine Country Inn & Restaurant

Healdsburg, California

An enchanting Victorian estate in the heart of Sonoma County's Dry Creek Valley, Madrona Manor offers luxurious accommodations, an acclaimed restaurant, and eight acres of lawns, gardens and woodlands. Almost immediately after driving through the property gate, guests feel they have transported themselves to a place where everyday worries can be left behind.

The three-story mansion was built in 1881 as a private residence for John Paxton, whose business enterprises included mining, banking, and lumber and who helped promote Sonoma County's fledgling wine industry. After Paxton's death, the property remained a private residence or sat vacant until 1981, when it was purchased and renovated to its present incarnation as a romantic country inn and restaurant. Bill and Trudi Konrad purchased Madrona Manor in 1999 and have completed an extensive restoration. Trudi Konrad has furnished the guest rooms and suites with an eclectic blend of folk art and European and Asian antiques to create an atmosphere of relaxed elegance.

Whether it's lounging by the swimming pool; reading in the Music Room with its rosewood piano; or relaxing with a glass of wine on the broad veranda; Madrona Manor provides a peaceful setting. Guests enjoy quiet strolls through the grounds, and during most of the year may even observe part of their evening meal growing in the organic kitchen garden. Each spring, Madrona's executive chef and head gardener confer over seed catalogs to choose vegetables for the garden, which includes more than twenty varieties of heirloom tomatoes during the summer.

Each morning there is a breakfast buffet, and in the evening, Madrona's romantic restaurant serves chef Jesse Mallgren's California cuisine in several lovely candlelit rooms of the house. The restaurant's wine list is strong on selections from the Alexander Valley, Russian River, and Dry Creek appellations and has been awarded *Wine Spectator* magazine's Award of Excellence. Madrona hosts a series of popular winemaker dinners throughout the year. Chef Mallgren meets with each winemaker and then creates a sequence of dishes that complements the flavors and fully reveals the nuances of each featured varietal.

Menu

Pear Salad with Watercress, Blue Cheese,
and Port Wine Vinaigrette

Navarro Gewürztraminer, 1998

❧

Pan-Seared Halibut with Spring Vegetable Ragout
and Olive Oil Mashed Potatoes

Preston Marsanne, 1998

❧

Peach and Blueberry Strudel
with Rose Petal Ice Cream

CHARLES BECK

Wine gives great pleasure, and every
pleasure, is of itself a good.

—SAMUEL JOHNSON

PEAR SALAD WITH WATERCRESS, BLUE CHEESE, AND PORT WINE VINAIGRETTE

The flavors of sweet pears, salty blue cheese, spicy greens, and vinaigrette balance perfectly in this stunning salad.

VINAIGRETTE

1 cup (8 fl oz/250 ml) ruby port
3 tablespoons red wine vinegar
1 tablespoon minced shallot
½ cup (8 fl oz/250 ml) extra-virgin olive oil
Salt and freshly ground pepper to taste

Leaves from 2 bunches frisée lettuce
2 bunches watercress, stemmed
2 ripe pears, peeled and cored
4 ounces (125 g) crumbled blue cheese, such as Maytag
1 tablespoon hazelnut oil (optional)

To make the vinaigrette: In a small, heavy saucepan, boil the port to reduce it to ¼ cup (2 fl oz/60 ml). Remove from heat and let cool. In a medium bowl, combine the port, vinegar, and shallot. Gradually whisk in the olive oil in a thin stream to make an emulsified sauce; season with salt and pepper.

Dice one of the pears. In a large bowl, combine the frisée, watercress, and diced pear. Add half of the vinaigrette and toss.

Arrange a mound of salad in the center of each of 4 plates and sprinkle with blue cheese.

Using a melon baller, scoop 12 balls from the remaining pear. Place 3 balls on each plate at the 1-o'clock, 6-o'clock, and 11-o'clock positions. Spoon the remaining vinaigrette over the salad, and drizzle the hazelnut oil, if using, around the edge of each plate.   *Makes 4 servings*

Pan-Seared Halibut with Spring Vegetable Ragout and Olive Oil Mashed Potatoes

Fresh, delicate spring vegetables are paired with mild-flavored halibut and served over a mound of mashed potatoes.

Spring Vegetable Ragout

2 pounds (1 kg) fava beans, shelled
½ bunch basil, stemmed
1/4 cup (2 fl oz/60 ml) canola oil
1½ cups (12 fl oz/375 ml) vegetable stock (see Basics) or
  canned vegetable broth
1 pound (500 g) green peas, shelled
2 tablespoons unsalted butter
Salt and freshly ground pepper to taste

4 halibut fillets, pin bones and skin removed
Salt and freshly ground pepper to taste
2 tablespoons canola oil
Olive Oil Mashed Potatoes (recipe follows)

To make the ragout: Blanch the fava beans in salted boiling water for 1 minute. Drain and rinse under cold water. Pinch open the end of each bean and pop it out of its skin.

Blanch the basil leaves in boiling water for 15 seconds. Drain, rinse under cold water, and squeeze out the excess moisture. In a blender or food processor, combine the basil and canola oil. Purée until smooth. Transfer to a fine-mesh sieve set over a bowl and drain. (Reserve the oil to use later in a salad dressing or to flavor vegetables).

Season both sides of the fillets with salt and pepper. In a large frying pan, heat the canola oil over medium-high heat until almost smoking. Add the fish and cook for 30 seconds, then reduce heat to medium and cook for about 3 minutes on each side, or until golden brown on the outside and opaque throughout.

Meanwhile, in a medium saucepan, combine the stock or broth, peas, and fava beans. Bring to a boil, reduce heat to low, and stir in the butter, 2 tablespoons of the basil purée, the salt, and pepper. Remove from heat.

Divide the ragout among 4 shallow bowls. Place a mound of mashed potatoes in the center of each bowl and top with a halibut fillet; serve immediately.   *Makes 4 servings*

Olive Oil Mashed Potatoes

4 Yukon Gold potatoes, peeled and diced
½ cup (4 fl oz/125 ml) milk
2 tablespoons unsalted butter
¼ cup (2 fl oz/60 ml) extra-virgin olive oil
Salt and freshly ground pepper to taste

Cook the potatoes in salted, boiling water for 5 to 10 minutes, or until tender. Drain. Press the potatoes through a ricer or mash them with a potato masher. In a small saucepan, combine the milk, butter, and olive oil. Heat over medium heat until the butter melts. Pour into the potatoes and stir lightly to blend. Season with salt and pepper. Set aside and keep warm. *Makes 4 servings*

Peach and Blueberry Strudel with Rose Petal Ice Cream

Filling

3 ripe peaches, peeled, pitted, and chopped
¼ cup (2 oz/60 g) sugar or to taste
½ cup (2 oz/60 g) fresh blueberries
¼ teaspoon each ground cinnamon, cloves, nutmeg, and ginger
⅛ teaspoon salt
½ teaspoon cornstarch
½ teaspoon flour
1 teaspoon unsalted butter, melted
¼ teaspoon vanilla extract
½ teaspoon fresh lemon juice
1 teaspoon orange juice

4 sheets thawed phyllo dough
2 tablespoons sugar mixed with ¼ teaspoon ground cinnamon
Rose Petal Ice Cream (recipe follows)

To make the filling: In a medium bowl, combine all the ingredients; set aside. Preheat the oven to 400°F (200°C). Lightly butter a baking sheet.

Stack the phyllo dough sheets and cut them into 4 crosswise strips. Brush 1 strip with melted butter and sprinkle with the cinnamon sugar. Top with another strip and brush with butter. Repeat, placing the strips at a right angle to form a cross. Repeat 3 times to make 4 crosses.

Place a spoonful of peach filling in the center of each cross and twist the edges to form pouches. Transfer the pouches to the prepared baking sheet and bake for 10 to 15 minutes, or until golden brown. Serve warm, with a scoop of rose petal ice cream alongside.   *Makes 4 servings*

ROSE PETAL ICE CREAM

Petals from 3 unsprayed roses
1½ cups (12 fl oz / 375 ml) heavy cream
1½ cups (12 fl oz / 375 ml) milk
¾ cup (6 oz / 185 g) sugar
3 egg yolks, lightly beaten
Rose water to taste

In a medium saucepan, combine the rose petals, cream, milk, and ¼ cup (2 oz / 60 g) of the sugar. Bring to a simmer over medium heat, stirring to dissolve the sugar. Remove from heat, cover, and set aside for 1 hour.

In a small bowl, whisk the remaining ½ cup (4 oz / 125 g) sugar and the egg yolks together until pale. Return the rose-flavored cream mixture to medium-low heat and bring to a simmer. Whisk 1 cup (8 fl oz / 250 ml) of the hot cream into the egg yolk mixture. Return the yolk mixture to the hot cream and cook over medium heat, stirring frequently, until thick enough to coat the back of a spoon. Strain the custard through a fine-meshed sieve and let cool. Cover and refrigerate for 2 hours to chill. Stir in the rose water. Freeze in an ice cream maker according to the manufacturer's instructions.
                    Makes 4 servings

The Maidstone Arms
Inn and Restaurant

East Hampton, New York

Just a short stroll from the center of East Hampton, with its galleries, boutiques, theater, and miles of magnificent beaches, Maidstone Arms offers Hamptons visitors historic charm, modern comfort, and elegant country dining. Dating back to 1740, the white clapboard structure has operated as an inn since the 1870s, when New York's social set established the Hamptons as a summer colony. An inn to enjoy in each season, Maidstone's front porch is decked out in wicker rocking chairs during the summer, and the charming back garden is a perfect place for sipping cooling ice teas. When winter arrives, Persian carpets are rolled out over the hardwood floors, fireplaces burn brightly in the cozy main sitting rooms, and guests head outdoors to ice skate on the pond across the street.

Maidstone's comfortable guest rooms and private cottages are decorated with original art and antique furnishings from around the world. Each morning begins with a continental breakfast of freshly baked breads, muffins, and scones served in the Water Room, and a more hearty English breakfast is available in the Boat Room. Guests enjoy a variety of sporting and leisure pursuits, including golf, tennis, riding, fishing, sailing, and visiting Long Island's acclaimed wineries.

The Maidstone Arms Restaurant, a cornerstone of the Hamptons' culinary scene, serves chef William S. Valentine's imaginative American cuisine. Born in Smithtown, Long Island, chef Valentine worked at New Orlean's Windsor Court Hotel and at Checkers Hotel Kempinski in Los Angeles before returning to his Long Island roots as the general manager and executive chef at Maidstone. Inspired in part by Sicilian, Southern, and Asian cooking, chef Valentine's seasonal menus balance exciting flavors and make full use of regional fish and game and locally-grown organic vegetables. Chef Valentine coordinates the inn's "Sunday Guest Chef" series, where he has cooked with great chefs such as Claude Troisgros, Gray Kunz, and Michael Romano. The restaurant's international wine list has received *Wine Spectator* magazine's Award of Excellence for the past seven years. Chef William Valentine created the following menu.

CASTELLO
di
BORGHESE

HARGRAVE VINEYARD

PINOT NOIR
1998

NORTH FORK OF LONG ISLAND

CABERNET
FRANC
SCHNEIDER
1998

NORTH FORK OF LONG ISLAND
ALC. 12.5 PERCENT BY VOLUME

L
PINOT BLANC
I
NORTH FORK
OF LONG ISLAND
E
1999
12.9% ALC / VOL
B

L
BLANC de BLANC
METHODE CHAMPENOISE SPARKLING WINE
I
NORTH FORK
OF LONG ISLAND
E
1993
12.5% ALC / VOL
B

BARREL FERMENTED
LENZ
GOLD LABEL
CHARDONNAY
NORTH FORK OF LONG ISLAND
1997

Wölffer

1998
The Hamptons, Long Island
ESTATE SELECTION
CHARDONNAY

ESTATE BOTTLED BY SAGPOND VINEYARDS
SAGAPONACK, NEW YORK, USA • ALC. 13.6% BY VOL. • 750 ML

1998   1998
PP
PALMER
Vineyards
North Fork of Long Island
MERLOT
PRODUCED & BOTTLED BY PALMER VINEYARDS
AQUEBOGUE, NEW YORK
Robert G Palmer
ALC. 12.8% BY VOL. 750 ML

DUCK WALK VINEYARDS
1997
CHARDONNAY
LONG ISLAND, NEW YORK
PRODUCED AND BOTTLED BY DUCK WALK VINEYARDS
WATER MILL, SOUTHAMPTON, N.Y. ALC. 12.5% BY VOL.

PELLEGRINI
VINEYARDS

NORTH FORK OF
LONG ISLAND
MERLOT
1997
UNFILTERED

Alcohol 13% by Volume

LAUREL LAKE
VINEYARDS
1998
North Fork of Long Island
Riesling
12.5% ALCOHOL BY VOLUME • 750ML

PAUMANOK
North Fork of Long Island
Chenin Blanc
2000
Dry Table Wine
Estate Bottled by
PAUMANOK Vineyards, Ltd.
Aquebogue, NY 11931

ESTATE BOTTLED
1997
Pugliese
Vineyards
Champagne
Blanc de Blanc
Brut
NORTH FORK OF LONG ISLAND
GROWN, PRODUCED AND BOTTLED BY
PUGLIESE VINEYARDS, INC.
CUTCHOGUE, LONG ISLAND, NEW YORK
ALC. 11.5% BY VOLUME CONTAINS SULFITES
750mL

Bedell Cellars
North Fork of Long Island
CABERNET
SAUVIGNON
1997

Menu

Smoked-Salmon Sushi

LIEB VINEYARDS BLANC DE BLANC MÉTHODE CHAMPENOISE, 1999

Spiced Rack of Lamb with
Curried Sweet Potatoes and Curry Sauce

SCHNEIDER CABERNET FRANC, 1998

Maple Pudding

WÖLFFER VINEYARDS LATE HARVEST CHARDONNAY, 1999

RALPH PUGLIESE, JR.

𝒜 man will be eloquent if you give him good wine. —RALPH WALDO EMERSON

1 cup (7 oz/220 g) short-grain rice
1½ cups (12 fl oz/375 ml) water
⅛ teaspoon salt
3 tablespoons rice vinegar
3 tablespoons sugar
⅛ teaspoon salt
1 tablespoon wasabi powder
8 ounces (250 g) smoked salmon, preferably Scottish-style
½ lemon, thinly sliced and cut into quarters
Soy sauce and thinly sliced pickled ginger for serving

Rinse the rice in 3 changes of water, stirring it with your hands to release the starch; drain well.

In a medium saucepan, combine the rice, water, and salt. Bring to a boil. Immediately cover, reduce heat to low, and simmer for 15 minutes. Remove from heat and let stand, covered, for 10 minutes. Transfer the rice to a large bowl.

In a small bowl, combine the rice vinegar, sugar, and salt. Pour the vinegar mixture over the hot rice and mix thoroughly with a vertical cutting motion. Cover the bowl with a damp cloth and let cool to room temperature.

Using your hands, roll the rice into balls about the diameter of a quarter. (If the rice sticks to your hands, dip them in a bowl of water). Dampen a 6-inch (15-cm) square piece of cheesecloth with water. In a small bowl, combine the wasabi powder with enough water to make a paste.

Place a dab of wasabi paste on top of each ball and top with a slice of salmon. Lay the damp cheesecloth over one of the balls and tighten, pressing so that the salmon adheres to the rice. With your finger, make a small indentation on top. Remove the cheesecloth and place another dab of wasabi in the indentation. Repeat to make 24 balls. Garnish each piece with a lemon quarter. Serve with soy sauce, pickled ginger, and chopsticks.   *Makes 24 balls; serves 4 to 6*

SPICED RACK OF LAMB WITH CURRIED SWEET POTATOES AND CURRY SAUCE

Chef Bill Valentine accompanies this sensational dish with pappadams (wafer-thin Indian flat breads made from lentil flour) and sautéed asparagus. Ask your butcher to "French" the rack, which means trimming the meat from the ends of the bone. For a flavorful vegetarian side dish, omit the lamb.

1 teaspoon salt
1 teaspoon ground pepper
½ teaspoon cayenne pepper
½ teaspoon sweet Hungarian paprika
½ teaspoon ground mace
½ teaspoon ground coriander
1 tablespoon olive oil
2 racks of lamb

CURRIED SWEET POTATOES

2 tablespoons peanut oil
1 red onion, diced
3 sweet potatoes, peeled and cut into ¾-inch (2-cm) dice
½-inch piece fresh ginger, peeled and minced
1 tablespoon curry powder
Salt and freshly ground pepper to taste
¼ cup (2 fl oz/60 ml) coconut milk
1 tablespoon chopped fresh cilantro

CURRY SAUCE

1 teaspoon peanut oil
½-inch piece fresh ginger, peeled and minced
2 shallots, minced
1 lemongrass stalk, white part only, peeled and chopped
2 red Thai chilies, seeded and minced
⅓ cup (½ oz/15 g) chopped cilantro stems
3 tablespoons curry powder
1 cup (8 fl oz/250 ml) dry sherry
2 cups (16 fl oz/500 ml) heavy cream or half-and-half
Salt and freshly ground pepper to taste

(continued on following page)

🍂 Preheat the oven to 450°F (230°C). In a small bowl, combine the salt and spices. Rub this mixture all over the lamb.

🍂 In a large ovenproof frying pan, add the olive oil and brown the lamb on all sides over medium heat, one rack at a time. Transfer to the oven and roast for 20 to 25 minutes, or until an instant-read thermometer inserted into the center of the lamb and not touching bone registers 125° to 130°F (52° to 54°C) for rare. Transfer to a platter and cover loosely with aluminum foil.

🍂 To make the sweet potatoes: In a large frying pan, heat the oil over medium heat and sauté the onion, sweet potatoes, ginger, curry, salt, and pepper for 10 minutes. Stir in the coconut milk and cilantro and sauté for 5 minutes, or until the sweet potatoes are tender.

🍂 To make the sauce: In a medium frying pan, heat the oil over medium-low heat and sauté the ginger, shallots, and lemongrass for 3 minutes. Add the chilies, cilantro stems, and curry and cook for 3 minutes over medium heat. Add the sherry, increase heat to high, and cook to reduce by half. Reduce heat to medium, add the cream, salt, and pepper, and cook until thick enough to coat the back of a spoon. Strain the sauce through a fine-mesh sieve, pressing on the solids with the back of a large spoon.

🍂 To serve, slice the lamb into chops. Place a mound of sweet potatoes in the center of each of 4 plates and spoon the sauce around them. Arrange 4 lamb chops around the sweet potatoes and serve immediately. *Makes 4 servings*

MAPLE PUDDING

Richly flavored and easy to make.

1 cup (8 fl oz/250 ml) heavy cream
¼ cup (3 oz/90 g) maple syrup
1 egg
3 egg yolks
Whipped cream for garnish

Preheat the oven to 325°F (165°C). In a small saucepan, combine the heavy cream and maple syrup. Whisk over medium-low heat until almost boiling. Turn off heat.

In a medium bowl, whisk the egg and egg yolks together until pale. Gradually whisk in the hot cream mixture. Pour the custard into four 4-ounce (125-ml) ramekins and transfer them to a baking dish. Pour hot water into the baking dish to reach halfway up the sides of the ramekins. Bake for 30 to 40 minutes, or until the puddings are set near the edges but jiggle slightly in the center when shaken. Remove from the oven and let cool. Refrigerate for at least 2 hours to chill. To serve, garnish with whipped cream, if desired.

Makes 4 servings

Meadowood Napa Valley

St. Helena, California

A secluded estate surrounded by 250 wooded acres, Meadowood is a center for social, cultural, and viticultural life in Napa Valley. Guests come to enjoy cultural and sporting activities, fine dining, and wine.

Once an exclusive private club, today it is a country resort with a full-service health spa, nine-hole golf course, seven tennis courts, and two championship croquet lawns. Meadowood's luxurious gabled cottages, suites, and lodges are tucked away in a preserve of open meadows, quiet woodlands, and naturalized gardens. Cultural events such as concerts, lectures, and seminars are held year-round at the resort, and guests can play croquet, golf, or tennis and hike, bicycle, run or swim—all on the estate grounds.

A wine-lover's delight, Meadowood offers tours of local vineyards, a Friday-night wine reception, an extraordinary cellar, and classes with the knowledgeable and entertaining John Thoreen, who professes the virtue of wine as "liquid poetry." Thoreen helps wine drinkers at every level gain personal insights into wine and confidence in their palate. At winemaker's dinners, he tells the story behind each wine and explains why it was chosen for the meal, and he might even read a poem or two before dinner concludes. Meadowood guests can enjoy spirited wine tasting games, cooking classes, visits to wineries not usually open to the public, and vineyard picnics. Meadowood hosts the Napa Valley Wine Auction.

The Restaurant at Meadowood showcases chef Steven Tevere's California wine country cuisine and has one of the most comprehensive lists of Napa Valley wines in the world. In pursuit of maximum flavor, chef Tevere bases his cooking on highest quality ingredients, polished technique, and a creative use of complementary flavors, with a special interest in food and wine pairing. The Grill at Meadowood offers California bistro food served in a casual atmosphere, and the Pool Terrace Café is open during summer months. The following recipes were created by chef Steven Tevere.

Menu

Dungeness Crab Salad with Meyer Lemon Vinaigrette

Voss Sauvignon Blanc, 1999

❧

Squab with Lentils and Braised Collard Greens

Anderson's Conn Valley Pinot Noir Valhalla Vineyard, 1997

❧

Crème Fraîche Panna Cotta with Huckleberry Sauce

Chappelet Moelleux, 1995

Mustard along Spring Street

Earl Thollander

EARL THOLLANDER

Wine has been a part of civilized life
for some seven thousand years.
It is the only beverage that feeds the
body, soul, and spirit of man and at
the same time stimulates the mind ...

—ROBERT MONDAVI

✿ DUNGENESS CRAB SALAD ✿
WITH MEYER LEMON VINAIGRETTE

Thin-skinned, mild-flavored Meyer lemons have a low-acid juice that complements the delicate sweetness of this crab salad.

CRAB SALAD

1 pound (500 g) fresh lump Dungeness crabmeat, picked over for shell
2 tablespoons finely chopped celery
2 tablespoons finely chopped red onion
2 tablespoons finely chopped peeled cucumber
2 tablespoons chopped mixed fresh herbs, such as parsley, tarragon, and basil
1 tablespoon fresh lemon juice
3 tablespoons mayonnaise
Salt and freshly ground pepper to taste

4 handfuls (4 oz / 125 g) mixed baby greens
Meyer Lemon Vinaigrette (recipe follows)
12 cherry tomatoes, halved
Leaves from 2 tarragon sprigs
Leaves from 2 flat-leaf parsley sprigs
2 tablespoons chopped fresh chives

❧ In a medium bowl, gently mix all the ingredients for the crab salad together. In another medium bowl, toss the mixed greens with ¼ cup (2 fl oz / 60 ml) of the vinaigrette until lightly dressed.

❧ Arrange a mound of mixed greens in the center of each of 4 plates. Fill an oiled 4-ounce (125-ml) ramekin with crab salad and unmold it over the greens. Spoon vinaigrette around each plate and garnish with the cherry tomatoes, tarragon, parsley, and chives; serve immediately.   *Makes 4 servings*

MEYER LEMON VINAIGRETTE

½ tablespoon Champagne vinegar
3 tablespoons Meyer lemon juice
⅓ cup (3 fl oz / 80 ml) extra-virgin olive oil
⅓ cup (3 fl oz / 80 ml) olive oil
Salt and freshly ground pepper to taste

❧ In a small bowl, whisk all the ingredients together. *Makes 1 cup (8 fl oz / 250 ml)*

SQUAB WITH LENTILS AND BRAISED COLLARD GREENS

A marvelous twist on an old bistro favorite, duck with lentils. If squab is unavailable, use Cornish game hens.

LENTILS

½ cup (3½ oz/105 g) French green lentils

1 teaspoon salt

¼ cup (2 fl oz/60 ml) chicken stock (see Basics) or canned low-salt
  chicken broth

½ tablespoon unsalted butter

Salt and freshly ground pepper to taste

BRAISED COLLARD GREENS

1 tablespoon unsalted butter

1 tablespoon olive oil

1 large onion, diced

2 ounces (60 g) pancetta, diced

1 bunch collard greens, chopped into 1-inch (2.5-cm) pieces

¾ cup (6 fl oz/180 ml) chicken stock or canned low-salt chicken broth

Salt and freshly ground pepper to taste

Leaves from 1 bunch thyme, minced

4 squabs, breasts and legs boned

Salt and freshly ground pepper to taste

1 tablespoon olive oil

½ cup (4 fl oz/125 ml) dry white wine

2 cups (16 fl oz/500 ml) chicken stock or canned low-salt chicken broth

1 tablespoon unsalted butter

To make the lentils: In a medium saucepan, combine the lentils, salt, and cold water to cover. Bring to a boil, reduce heat to low, and simmer for 15 minutes. Drain the lentils and return them to the saucepan. Stir in the stock or broth, butter, salt, and pepper.

To make the greens: In a large, heavy saucepan, melt the butter with the olive oil over medium-low heat and sauté the onion for 3 minutes. Add the pancetta and sauté until crisp. Add the greens, stock or broth, salt, and pepper. Cover and simmer for 8 to 10 minutes; remove from heat and set aside.

Open up the squabs and flatten the breastbones with the heel of your hand. Sprinkle with salt and pepper. In a large frying pan, heat the olive oil over medium heat and sear the squab, skin side down, for 4 minutes. Reduce heat to medium, turn the squab over, and cook for 1 minute. Transfer to a plate and cover loosely with aluminum foil.

Pour off all the oil from the pan. Pour in the wine and stir to scrape up any browned bits from the bottom of the pan. Increase heat to high and cook to reduce by half. Pour in the stock or broth and cook to reduce by half. Whisk in the butter and season with salt and pepper to taste.

Stir the thyme into the braised greens. Spoon a mound of lentils into the center of each of 4 warmed plates. Surround the lentils with braised greens and place a squab on top of the lentils. Spoon some sauce around the lentils and serve immediately.   *Makes 4 servings*

CRÈME FRAÎCHE PANNA COTTA WITH HUCKLEBERRY SAUCE

Rich, tangy, smooth, not too sweet—the first bite of this "cooked cream" will make you close your eyes and savor the moment. Huckleberry sauce made with port is a perfect foil. If huckleberries are unavailable, blueberries are also delicious.

PANNA COTTA
2 tablespoons water
1 teaspoon plain gelatin
½ cup (4 fl oz/125 ml) heavy cream
2 tablespoons sugar
1 cup (8 oz/250 g) crème fraîche*
¼ cup (2 oz/60 g) mascarpone cheese**

HUCKLEBERRY SAUCE
¾ cup (6 oz/185 g) sugar
1 cup (8 fl oz/250 ml) water
½ cup (4 fl oz/125 ml) port
1 cup (4 oz/125 g) fresh huckleberries or fresh or thawed frozen blueberries
4 mint sprigs for garnish

In a small saucepan, combine the water and gelatin. Stir over low heat until the gelatin dissolves, about 5 minutes; remove from heat.

In a double boiler over simmering water, combine the cream, sugar, crème fraîche, and mascarpone. Whisk together until smooth and hot. Remove from heat and stir in the dissolved gelatin. Pour into four 4-ounce (125-ml) ramekins. Let cool, then refrigerate for at least 6 hours or overnight before serving.

To make the sauce: In a medium saucepan, combine the sugar and water and stir over medium heat until dissolved. Add the port and half of the huckleberries. Reduce heat to low and cook for 20 minutes. Transfer to a blender or food processor and purée. Strain through a fine-mesh sieve back into the saucepan. Add the remaining huckleberries and cook over medium heat for 3 to 4 minutes. Transfer to a small bowl and let cool. Cover and refrigerate for at least 1 hour to chill.

To serve, run a paring knife around the inside of each ramekin and unmold the panna cotta onto a dessert plate, tapping the bottom of the ramekin. Spoon the huckleberry sauce over the panna cotta and around the plate. Insert a mint sprig into the panna cotta and serve.   *Makes 4 servings*

*Crème fraîche is a lightly soured cream available in many grocery stores and specialty foods stores. To make your own, see Basics.

**Mascarpone, a delicately flavored triple-cream cheese from Lombardy, is available in many grocery stores and most Italian foods stores.

Oak Knoll Inn

Napa, California

Driving past vineyards down a tree-lined avenue crossing gorgeous Napa Valley, it is easy to miss Oak Knoll's simple stone building hidden behind a wall of cypress. Guests enter by way of a charming reception area and are immediately drawn to a spacious outdoor deck with magnificent views of the inn's pool and garden, 600 acres of surrounding vineyards, and Stags Leap Mountain beyond. Barbara and John Passino have created an elegant private retreat where guests feel they can drop all cares and just enjoy themselves.

Oak Knoll's guest rooms have double stone walls, private entrances, and wood burning fireplaces, which all contribute to a sense of intimacy. A refreshing splash in the pool and a soothing soak in the Jacuzzi are delightful ways to begin and end the day. Barbara Passino and her staff can help guests plan itineraries that may include visits to wineries that require appointments, picnic arrangements, balloon rides, and bicycle tours. Art galleries, museums, antique shops, boutiques, fishing, horseback riding, and golfing are all available nearby, and some of Napa's best-known restaurants and wineries are just minutes away; in fact, more than 250 wineries are within a twenty-minute radius.

Guests assemble in the early evening for a reception and enjoy selected wines with delicious hors d'oeuvres. A local winemaker often pours, answering questions and presenting a fun, informative discussion.

Each morning begins with an extravagant breakfast served in courses. This leisurely feast is enjoyed outside on the sunny deck during warm months or in front of a crackling fire on nippy winter mornings. The following menu is Barbara Passino's salute to the Mexican heritage of many people who work in the vineyards and bring in the harvest.

STEVEN GORDON

Drinking wine is just a part of life,
like eating food.

—FRANCIS FORD COPPOLA, MOVIEMAKER AND WINE COLLECTOR

North of Southwest
Breakfast Menu

Chocolate Tacos with Fresh Fruit

❧

Chiles Unrellenos with Salsa Fresca

❧

Black Velvet Beans

❧

Corn Bread Muffins

CHOCOLATE TACOS WITH FRESH FRUIT

While chocolate tacos may sound decadent, this is actually a low-cholesterol recipe. The dark chocolate tortillas provide a nice texture and flavor contrast to the sweetness of seasonal fresh fruit and an icy fruit sorbet.

CHOCOLATE TORTILLAS

⅓ cup (3 fl oz/80 ml) low-fat milk

2 large egg whites

¼ cup (2 fl oz/60 ml) canola oil

½ cup (2½ oz/75 g) all-purpose flour

½ cup (4 oz/125 g) sugar

3 tablespoons unsweetened cocoa powder

1½ teaspoons vanilla extract

¼ teaspoon salt

2 cups (8 oz/250 g) fresh strawberries, hulled, sliced, and sprinkled with a little black pepper

½ cup (2 oz/60 g) fresh raspberries

½ cup (2 oz/60 g) fresh blackberries

½ cup (2 oz/60 g) fresh blueberries

1 mango, peeled and cut into ½-inch (12-mm) dice (see Basics)

1 kiwi, peeled and sliced into rounds

1 small banana, peeled and sliced into rounds just before serving

½ pint (8 oz/250 g) strawberry or other fruit sorbet

4 mint sprigs

4 edible flowers such as nasturtium or pansies (optional)

To make the tortillas: In a blender or food processor, combine all the ingredients and process until smooth. Cover and refrigerate for at least 2 hours or overnight.

Remove the batter from the refrigerator 30 minutes before cooking. Heat an 8-inch (20-cm) nonstick or seasoned crêpe pan over medium heat; if using a seasoned pan, brush with oil. Stir the batter and pour a scant ¼ cupful (2 fl oz/60 ml) into the pan. Immediately tilt the pan to spread the batter in a circle. Cook for about 1 minute, or until the edges look dry, then loosen with a rubber spatula or your fingers and turn over. Cook for 1 or 2 minutes on the other side.

Lift the tortilla out of the pan and quickly drape it over a rolling pin. It will become firm as it cools. Repeat to cook the remaining batter.

In a medium bowl, combine the strawberries, raspberries, blackberries, and blueberries. Gently mix.

To serve, fill each tortilla generously with berries. Tuck in the mango, kiwi, and bananas. Add a scoop of sorbet on top of the fruit, garnish with a mint sprig and a flower, if using, and serve immediately. *Makes 4 servings*

 CHILES UNRELLENOS

Assembled like a spanakopita, but using chilies and jack cheese, chiles unrellenos are served hot out of the oven as part of this Southwestern breakfast. For lunch, they could be served at room temperature with a green salad.

4 poblano or Anaheim chilies, roasted and peeled (see Basics), or canned
    whole green chilies, rinsed
4 eggs
1 cup (8 fl oz/250 ml) heavy cream
½ teaspoon salt
½ teaspoon cumin seeds, toasted in a small frying pan until fragrant
1 tablespoon unsalted butter, melted
1 tablespoon canola oil
8 sheets thawed frozen phyllo dough, cut in half crosswise
2 cups (8 oz/250 g) diced Sonoma or Monterey jack cheese
¼ cup (1 oz/30 g) freshly grated Parmesan or dry jack cheese
Salsa Fresca (recipe follows)

Preheat the oven to 450°F (230°C). Tear the chilies lengthwise into strips 2 inches (5 cm) wide. In a medium bowl, beat the eggs, cream, and salt together.

In a small bowl, combine the melted butter and oil and brush a little on the bottom and sides of an 8-inch (20-cm) square baking dish. Arrange a layer of phyllo on the bottom of the baking dish and lightly brush with the butter mixture. Repeat to make 3 more phyllo layers. Place the chili strips evenly over the phyllo and evenly sprinkle with the diced and grated cheese. Pour in the egg mixture and sprinkle with the cumin seeds. Top with the remaining 12 layers of phyllo, brushing each layer with the butter mixture.

Using a sharp knife, score the phyllo into 4 serving pieces by cutting through 6 or 7 layers; do not cut all the way through to the filling, or the phyllo will become soggy. (These scores make the dish easier to cut after baking.)

Bake for 20 minutes. Reduce the oven temperature to 350°F (180°C) and bake for an additional 25 to 30 minutes, or until a knife inserted in the center comes out clean. Let cool for 5 minutes, then slice and serve with the salsa alongside.

Makes 4 servings

SALSA FRESCA

A fiery, flavorful salsa that works well with the mild quiche. For a milder salsa, omit the habanero.

4 tomatoes, diced
1 jalapeno chili, seeded and minced
1 habanero chili, seeded and minced (optional)
½ red onion, finely chopped
¼ cup (⅓ oz / 10 g) minced fresh cilantro
Salt and freshly ground pepper to taste
Juice of ½ lime, or more to taste

In a medium bowl, combine the tomato, jalapeno, optional habanero, red onion, and cilantro. Let sit for 15 minutes. Drain off any excess liquid. Stir in the salt, pepper, and lime juice.   *Makes about 2 cups (16 oz / 500 g)*

BLACK VELVET BEANS

Epazote, an herb that grows easily in the garden or in pots, is traditionally added to black beans in Mexico, both for its flavor and because it is a carminative.

1 cup (7 oz/220 g) dried black beans, picked over and rinsed*
1 onion, coarsely chopped
2 garlic cloves, smashed
1 large sprig epazote, or 1½ teaspoons dried** (optional)
1 tablespoon minced fresh thyme, or 1 teaspoon dried thyme
1 serrano chili, seeded and minced
Salt to taste
Sour cream for garnish

In a large saucepan, combine the beans, onion, garlic, epazote (if using), thyme, and chili. Add water to cover the beans by 1 inch (2.5 cm). Bring to a boil. Immediately reduce heat to low, partially cover, and simmer for 2 hours, or until tender. Add boiling water as necessary to keep the beans covered while cooking.

Drain the beans, reserving the broth. In a blender or food processor, purée the beans, ½ cup (4 fl oz/125 ml) of the reserved broth, and the salt. Add more broth if needed for consistency. Transfer the purée to a serving bowl, swirl in some sour cream, and serve at once.   *Makes 4 servings*

*Two 15-ounce (425 g) cans cooked black beans may be used instead of the dried beans, in which case drain, rinse, and then simmer for 20 minutes.

**Epazote is available at many specialty foods stores or by mail from Penzey's (see Resources).

🍇 CORN BREAD MUFFINS 🍇

Moist muffins that complement the Southwestern flavors of this menu.

1 cup (5 oz/155 g) all-purpose flour
1 cup (5 oz/155 g) cornmeal
¼ cup (2 oz/60 g) sugar
1 tablespoon baking powder
½ teaspoon salt
1 teaspoon cumin seeds, toasted in a small frying pan until fragrant
1 egg
1 cup (8 fl oz/250 ml) milk
5 tablespoons (2½ oz/75 g) unsalted butter, melted
½ cup (3 oz/90 g) fresh or thawed frozen corn kernels, blanched for 1 minute

🍃 Preheat the oven to 400°F (200°C). Butter 12 muffin cups.

🍃 In a large bowl, combine the flour, cornmeal, sugar, baking powder, salt, and cumin seeds. Stir well. In a small bowl, beat the egg, milk, and butter until blended. Stir the wet ingredients and corn into the dry ingredients just until mixed; the batter should be slightly lumpy.

🍃 Spoon the batter into the prepared cups and bake for 20 to 25 minutes, or until a skewer inserted in the center of a muffin comes out clean.

Makes 12 muffins

Oak Knoll Inn

Rose Inn

Ithaca, New York

Known locally as "the house with the circular staircase," this Italianate mansion offers elegance, comfort, and relaxation in the heart of New York's magnificent Finger Lakes region. Owners Charles and Sherry Rosemann have created New York's only Mobil Four-Star and AAA Four-Star country inn.

Built on the eastern side of Cayuga Lake in about 1850, the Rose Inn sits amid ten acres of lawns, apple orchards, and formal gardens. The central feature of the house is its famed circular staircase of highly polished Honduras mahogany, which spirals up three floors to a cupola and is decorated with inlaid marquetry floors and newel post. Sherry Rosemann has furnished the inn's guest rooms and suites with lush fabrics, folk art, and antiques.

Each morning guests enjoy a magnificent country breakfast that includes Sherry's homemade jams and preserves, seasonal local fruits, and a choice of two main dishes. Since fifteen varieties of apples are picked from the Rose Inn's apple orchard, homemade apple cider is often poured. Guests enjoy tours and wine tastings at nearby Finger Lakes wineries, antiquing, golfing, fishing, sailing, hiking, and visiting the campuses of nearby Cornell University and Ithaca and Wells Colleges.

Dinner is served in the Carriage House, a structure built in 1842 that is located at the side of the property. With its original interior barn siding, hand-hewn chestnut beams, and polished oak flooring, the restaurant is a wonderful setting for romantic candlelight dining. On weekends, the restaurant becomes the Carriage House Jazz Club, offering French-influenced seasonal menus and live jazz performances by local musicians. During the month of March, the Rose Inn hosts a popular series of winemaker dinners. Guests meet outstanding New York vintners and enjoy a four-course dinner that is created to pair with the winemaker's selections.

Menu

Composed Salad with Raspberry Dressing

WAGNER WINERY GEWÜRZTRAMINER, 1999

&

Salmon Fillet with Pink Grapefruit Beurre Blanc

WAGNER WINERY RIESLING, 1999

&

Poached Pears with Red Wine Caramel Sauce

KRISTIAN S. REYNOLDS

Pour it and they will come. —PROFESSOR STEVEN MUTKOSKI

*(Professor at Cornell University's School of Hotel Administration,
when asked how he maintains year after year a class size of over
800 students for his Wine and Spirits Class)*

Composed Salad with Raspberry Dressing

The colors and shapes in this salad create a feast for the eyes as well as the mouth.

20 snow peas, trimmed
1 head Bibb or Boston lettuce
2 tomatoes, cut into 8 wedges
4 hearts of palm, cut into rounds ¼ inch (6 mm) thick
4 cooked artichoke hearts (see Basics) or canned artichokes
1 each red and yellow bell pepper, seeded, deribbed, and cut into 4 thin rings
4 small handfuls onion or alfalfa sprouts, ends trimmed evenly
4 fresh edible flowers such as pansies or nasturtiums for garnish (optional)
Raspberry Dressing (recipe follows)

Blanch the snow peas in boiling water for 1 minute. Drain and rinse under cold running water; pat dry.

On each of 4 plates, arrange lettuce leaves in an overlapping circle with the stem ends towards the center. Fan 4 tomato wedges on top, pointing towards the outside of the plate. Arrange the heart of palm slices next to the tomatoes and fan out 5 snow peas. Place 1 artichoke heart next to the snow peas and top with a red pepper ring. Place a yellow pepper ring over the tomatoes. Arrange the sprouts in the center, pulling them apart so they resemble a flower. Top the sprouts with a flower, if using. Serve immediately and drizzle with the raspberry dressing at the table. *Makes 4 servings*

Raspberry Dressing

2 tablespoons raspberry vinegar
½ tablespoon Dijon mustard
1 egg yolk (see Note)
½ teaspoon salt
¼ teaspoon freshly ground pepper
1 teaspoon sugar
2 fresh basil leaves
⅓ cup (3 fl oz/80 ml) extra-virgin olive oil

In a blender or food processor, combine the vinegar, mustard, egg yolk, salt, pepper, sugar, and basil. Purée until smooth. With the machine running, gradually add the olive oil in a thin stream to make an emulsified sauce. Refrigerate. *Makes about ⅔ cup (6 fl oz/180 ml)*

Note: If you are concerned about eating uncooked eggs, omit the egg yolk.

SALMON FILLET WITH
PINK GRAPEFRUIT BEURRE BLANC

An elegant, delicately-flavored main course. Pour a glass of chilled Riesling and enjoy.

PINK GRAPEFRUIT BEURRE BLANC

2 tablespoons dry white wine, plus ¾ cup (6 fl oz/180 ml)
¼ cup (2 oz/60 g) sugar
½ cup (4 fl oz/125 ml) fresh pink grapefruit juice
2 shallots, minced
¼ cup (2 fl oz/60 ml) white wine vinegar
½ cup (4 fl oz/125 ml) heavy cream
1 cup (8 oz/250 g) cold unsalted butter, diced
Salt to taste

4 salmon fillets, pin bones removed but skin intact
¼ cup (2 oz/60 g) clarified butter, melted (see Basics)
Salt and freshly ground pepper to taste
2 tablespoons unsalted butter
2 bunches spinach, stemmed and rinsed
1 pink grapefruit, peeled and segmented (see Basics)
Diced candied grapefruit peel for garnish (optional); see Basics

🍃 Prepare a fire in an outdoor grill or preheat the broiler.

🍃 To make the beurre blanc: In a medium saucepan, combine the 2 table-spoons wine and the sugar and cook over medium-high heat, stirring until the sugar dissolves. Boil, without stirring, until the liquid caramelizes to a light brown. Using a wooden spoon, stir in the grapefruit juice and cook until reduced to a syrup that lightly coats the back of a spoon.

🍃 In a small saucepan, combine the shallots, ¾ cup (6 fl oz/180 ml) wine, and the vinegar. Boil until reduced to 1 tablespoon. Reduce heat to low and whisk in the cream, then whisk in the butter 1 tablespoon at a time. Remove from heat and season with salt. Stir in the grapefruit juice mixture. Cover and keep warm over tepid water.

❧ Brush each salmon fillet with clarified butter and sprinkle with salt and pepper. Place the fillets, skin side down, on the grill or place, skin side up, under the broiler. Cook for 3 to 4 minutes, then turn and cook on the second side for 3 to 4 minutes, or until the fish is opaque on the outside and just slightly translucent in the center. Transfer to a plate.

❧ Meanwhile, in a large frying pan, melt the butter over medium-high heat until the foam begins to subside. Add the spinach and cook, stirring, until it wilts; remove from heat. Cover to keep warm.

❧ Carefully peel the skin from the salmon. Arrange a nest of spinach on one side of each of 4 warmed plates and spoon some beurre blanc on the other side of the plate. Place a salmon fillet across the sauce and the spinach. Garnish the spinach with pink grapefruit segments and sprinkle candied grapefruit peel, if using, over the salmon; serve immediately. *Makes 4 servings*

Poached Pears with Red Wine Caramel Sauce

Prepare the pears 1 or 2 days before you plan to serve them.

3 cups (24 fl oz/750 ml) port
1 cup (8 oz/250 g) sugar
2 star anise
1 cinnamon stick
6 cloves
1 nutmeg
Stripped zest of 1 lemon
2 Bartlett or Anjou pears, peeled, halved, and cored

Red Wine Caramel Sauce

1 cup (8 oz/250 g) sugar
¼ cup (2 fl oz/60 ml) water
¼ cup (2 fl oz/60 ml) dry red wine
½ cup (4 fl oz/125 ml) heavy cream
1 tablespoon unsalted butter
Pinch of salt

In a medium saucepan, bring the port, sugar, star anise, cinnamon, cloves, nutmeg, and lemon zest to a boil. Reduce heat to medium-low. Add the pears and enough water to barely cover them. Cook just below simmering for 20 minutes, or until the pears are tender.

Using a slotted spoon, transfer the pears to a medium bowl. Cook the poaching liquid over high heat until reduced by half. Pour the poaching liquid over the pears to completely cover them. Let cool. Cover and refrigerate for at least 1 or up to 2 days.

To make the sauce: In a medium saucepan, combine the sugar, water, and wine. Bring to a boil and cook until caramel in color. Remove from heat and stir in ¼ cup (2 fl oz/60 ml) of the cream and the butter. Cook over low heat for 5 minutes. Remove from heat and let cool to room temperature. Stir in the remaining ¼ cup (2 fl oz/60 ml) cream and the salt.

To serve, place a pear half in each of 4 bowls or goblets. Rewarm the caramel sauce over low heat. Spoon over the pears.   *Makes 4 servings*

Rose Inn

Simpson House Inn

Santa Barbara, California

Built in 1874 by Scotsman Robert Simpson, this elegant Victorian estate is surrounded by an acre of lovely gardens and just a short stroll from downtown Santa Barbara, one of the most beautiful cities in the world. The estate's distinguished house, 1878 barn, and three English-style garden cottages have been lovingly restored and built by Glyn and Linda Davies, who have created North America's only AAA Five Diamond bed and breakfast inn.

The Davies family undertook the tremendous task of restoring the historic Victorian as their family home, and in 1976 they began scraping off layers of paint from the oak floors, installing windows, finding antique doors, ceiling moldings and fixtures, and adding a foundation. In 1985, the Simpson House opened its doors as a gracious bed and breakfast inn, and in 1992 the house and gardens were declared a historic landmark. The following year the couple added three luxurious garden cottages that have charming private courtyards with trickling fountains. Guests rooms are now available in the Victorian mansion, the carefully restored barn, and the garden cottages.

Within walking distance of Simpson House, are the Santa Barbara mission, museums, restaurants, theaters, and shops, and within a short drive are botanical gardens, beaches, windsurfing, sailing, horseback riding, hiking and picnicking. Spa services such as aromatherapy, massage, and skincare are available in the privacy of the inn's rooms, suites, and cottages. Simpson House makes a wonderful home-base for visiting the many excellent wineries of the Santa Ynez valley, and in the afternoon guests enjoy a convivial tasting of selected Santa Barbara county wines with a sumptuous array of Mediterranean appetizers.

Each morning a leisurely gourmet breakfast is served in the formal dining room of the main house or on the wrap-around veranda overlooking the gardens. Highlights include fresh organic California juices, seasonal fresh fruits, housemade granola, and a choice of house specialties such as crêpes and French toast.

Breakfast Menu

Simpson House Juleps

❧

Honeydew Melon with Basil Chiffonade

❧

Candied-Ginger Scones

❧

Asiago-Mushroom Crêpes

SIMPSON HOUSE JULEPS

A delightful way to begin the day.

Ice cubes
4 cups (32 fl oz/1 l) fresh orange juice
1 cup (8 fl oz/250 ml) soda water or sparkling mineral water
8 fresh mint leaves, chopped
Sugar for coating
4 mint sprigs

Fill a pitcher with ice cubes and add the orange juice, water, and mint. Stir to blend. Dip the rims of 4 wineglasses in a shallow bowl of water. Dip each glass into a plate of sugar to coat the rims. Carefully pour the julep into the prepared glasses. Garnish each drink with a mint sprig. *Makes 4 drinks*

Bronze is the mirror of the form; wine, of the heart.

—AESCHYLUS

HONEYDEW MELON WITH BASIL CHIFFONADE

½ cup (¾ oz/20 g) fresh basil leaves
1 honeydew melon, seeded, peeled, and cut into ¾-inch (2-cm) dice

❧ Stack the basil leaves in batches and cut them crosswise into fine shreds. Divide the melon among 4 shallow Champagne glasses. Sprinkle with basil.

Makes 4 servings

CANDIED GINGER SCONES

Ginger-lovers will adore these scones.

3 cups (15 oz/470 g) all-purpose flour
2 tablespoons baking powder
¾ teaspoon salt
1⅛ cups (2¼ oz/65 g) diced candied ginger
1¾ cups (14 fl oz/430 ml) plus 2 tablespoons heavy cream
2 tablespoons unsalted butter, melted
3 tablespoons sugar

❧ Preheat the oven to 425°F (220°C). In a large bowl, combine the flour, baking powder, and salt. Add the ginger and cream and stir until the dough holds together in a rough mass; it will be quite sticky.
❧ On a lightly floured surface, knead the dough 8 or 9 times. Divide into 15 portions and pat each portion into a circle. Brush the tops with the melted butter and sprinkle with sugar. Transfer to an ungreased baking sheet and bake in the preheated oven for 15 minutes, or until crusty and lightly golden. Serve warm.

Makes 15 scones

ASIAGO MUSHROOM CRÊPES

CRÊPES
½ cup (2½ oz/45 g) all-purpose flour
½ cup (4 fl oz/125 ml) milk
¼ cup (2 fl oz/60 ml) lukewarm water
2 eggs
2 tablespoons unsalted butter, melted
1 teaspoon salt

ASIAGO RICOTTA FILLING
1 cup (4 oz/125 g) grated Asiago cheese
15 ounces (470 g) ricotta cheese

SAUTÉED MUSHROOMS
1½ tablespoons unsalted butter
6 ounces (185 g) mushrooms, thinly sliced

2 tablespoons unsalted butter, melted
Cheese Sauce (recipe follows)

To make the crêpes: In a blender or food processor, combine all the ingredients and blend until smooth, stopping the machine to scrape down the sides once or twice. Cover and refrigerate for at least 2 hours or for up to 2 days.

To make the filling: In a large bowl, stir the cheeses together to blend.

Heat an 8-inch (20-cm) nonstick or seasoned crêpe pan over medium heat until a drop of water flicked on the surface jumps around. Brush the seasoned crêpe pan with melted butter. Stir the batter and pour in a scant ¼ cupful (2 fl oz/60 ml). Immediately tilt the pan to spread the batter evenly. Cook until the edge of the crêpe is dry, about 1 minute. Loosen with a plastic spatula or your fingers and flip it over. Cook for about 1 minute. Transfer the crêpe to a plate. Repeat, stacking the crêpes.

To sauté the mushrooms: In a large frying pan, melt the butter over medium-high heat until the foam subsides. Add the mushrooms and sauté until slightly browned.

Spoon a scant ¼ cup (2 oz/60 g) of the filling into the center of each crêpe. Fold the edges of each crêpe over the filling to form a rectangle.

In a large frying pan, melt the 2 tablespoons butter over medium heat until the foam subsides. Add the crêpes and cook until golden brown on both sides. Arrange 2 crêpes on each of 6 warmed plates, spoon over some sauce and mushrooms, and serve immediately. *Makes 6 servings*

CHEESE SAUCE

2½ cups (20 fl oz/625 ml) milk
½ onion
Salt and freshly ground pepper to taste
4 tablespoons (2 oz/60 g) unsalted butter
¼ cup (1½ oz/45 g) flour
½ cup (2 oz/60 g) grated Asiago cheese

In a small saucepan, combine the milk, onion, salt, and pepper. Bring to a simmer over low heat and cook for 15 minutes. Remove the onion.

In a medium, heavy saucepan, melt the butter over medium heat. Add the flour and stir for 2 minutes, or until fragrant but not browned. Remove from heat and gradually whisk in the milk mixture. Return to heat and simmer, whisking often, for 5 to 8 minutes, or until thickened. Stir in the cheese, and salt and pepper to taste. Cook until the cheese melts. Remove from heat and keep warm. *Makes about 2 cups (16 fl oz/500 ml)*

SUE TREUHAFT

Sonoma Mission Inn & Spa

Sonoma, California

Originally a sacred healing ground for the Miwok Indians, who were drawn by the curative powers of its underground springs, this famous spa resort offers luxurious accommodations, two award-winning restaurants, and ten acres of lushly planted grounds. The spa has been completely rebuilt for the new century and a full repertoire of massages, facials, fragrant herbal wraps, and holistic practices from different cultures are intended to soothe, beautify, and revitalize. Sonoma Mission's historic golf course has been expertly restored to provide a challenging championship course in beautiful Sonoma wine country.

Built in 1927 as an architectural reproduction of a California Mission, complete with bell tower, arcade, and red tile roof, the inn itself underwent a major restoration in 1980, and in 1993 the legendary underground hot springs were brought back to the surface to fill the spa pools with 135°F (57°C) mineral water. Sonoma Mission Inn has been awarded four stars by Mobil and four diamonds by AAA and was named Best Resort Spa in the World by *Gourmet* magazine.

Executive chef Toni Robertson's fresh, sophisticated California cuisine is served in the casually elegant Sonoma Mission Restaurant. Chef Robertson has previously worked at the Pan Pacific in Singapore, at the Palace in South Africa, and at the Grand Wailea in Maui, and her cooking reflects global influences while highlighting Sonoma county produce, meats, poultry, and seafood. Throughout the year the restaurant offers a series of winemaker dinners that pair the region's top producers with menus by the talented chef. The wine list, honored with *Wine Spectator* magazine's Best of Award of Excellence, features over 300 Sonoma Valley and Napa Valley wines. Sonoma Mission's casual Big 3 Diner, serving hearty country breakfasts and eclectic American cuisine for lunch and dinner, has been a favorite with locals for more than fifty years. Chef Toni Robertson created the following dinner menu for Menus and Music.

Menu

Scallop and Pea Shoot Dumplings
in Fresh Tomato Broth

MATANZAS CREEK SAUVIGNON BLANC

❧

Herb and Spice–Crusted Beef Tenderloin
with Black Bean Rice Cakes and Spicy Mango Salsa

HANZELL PINOT NOIR

❧

Warm Mission Fig Kabobs
with Honey and Buttermilk Sherbet

Kay Carlson

Nothing more excellent or valuable than wine was ever granted by the gods to man. —Plato

SCALLOP AND PEA SHOOT DUMPLINGS IN FRESH TOMATO BROTH

Easily prepared and beautifully presented, this light appetizer takes full advantage of fresh spring ingredients. Make the tomato broth 1 day before serving.

8 sea scallops
⅓ cup (½ oz/15 g) fresh pea shoots
⅔ cup (½ oz/15 g) baby spinach leaves
1½ teaspoons minced fresh ginger
1½ teaspoons finely chopped green onion
8 fresh basil leaves
Salt and freshly ground pepper to taste
4 round wonton skins
Minced fresh flat-leaf parsley or fresh chives cut into
   1-inch (2.5-cm) pieces for garnish
Tomato Broth (recipe follows)

To make the dumplings: Reserve 4 of the scallops. Slice the remaining scallops in half horizontally. Set aside.

Blanch the pea shoots and spinach in boiling water for 30 seconds; drain. Let cool and squeeze dry. In a blender or food processor, combine the pea shoots, spinach, ginger, green onion, basil, salt, pepper, and the 4 reserved scallops; process to make a slightly course purée.

On a work surface, lay out a wrapper and place a small dollop of purée in the center. Top with a sea scallop half, another dollop of purée, and another scallop half. Pinch the wrapper around the edges of the top scallop half to create an open-faced dumpling. Repeat to create 3 more dumplings.

In a covered steamer over boiling water, cook the dumplings for 5 to 6 minutes, or just until the exposed scallops are opaque.

Arrange a dumpling in each of 4 shallow soup bowls and spoon in the tomato broth. Garnish each dumpling with parsley or chives and serve immediately.

Serves 4 as an appetizer

TOMATO BROTH

4 tomatoes, preferably yellow, peeled (see Basics)
1 small shallot, minced
1 garlic clove, minced
½ cup (4 fl oz/125 ml) vegetable stock (see Basics) or
   canned vegetable broth
Salt and freshly ground pepper to taste

In a blender or food processor, combine the tomatoes, shallot, garlic, and stock or broth. Purée until smooth. Add salt and pepper. Strain through a fine-mesh sieve set over a bowl. Refrigerate overnight, letting the liquid drain. (Do not force it through, or it will become cloudy).

Just before serving, heat in a small saucepan over medium-low heat until warm. *Makes about 1 cup (8 fl oz/250 ml)*

HERB AND SPICE–CRUSTED BEEF TENDERLOIN WITH BLACK BEAN RICE CAKES AND SPICY MANGO SALSA

SPICY MANGO SALSA

1 mango, peeled and diced (see Basics)
1 tomato, seeded and chopped (see Basics)
2 tablespoons finely diced onion
1 jalapeno chili, seeded and minced
1 tablespoon minced fresh cilantro
Juice of 1 lemon
Salt and freshly ground pepper to taste

¼ cup (1 oz/30 g) mixed coriander seeds, black peppercorns, and fennel seeds
2 tablespoons salt
2 tablespoons packed brown sugar
2 tablespoons minced fresh flat-leaf parsley
2 tablespoons minced fresh chives
1 pound (500 g) beef tenderloin
1 tablespoon olive oil
Black Bean Rice Cakes (recipe follows)

To make the salsa: In a medium bowl, combine all the ingredients. Set aside to let the flavors blend.

In a spice grinder or a mortar, grind the coriander, peppercorns, and fennel seeds. In a small bowl, mix the ground spices, salt, sugar, parsley, and chives together. Rub the beef on both sides with the mixture. Cover with plastic wrap or place in a plastic bag and set aside at room temperature for 2 hours.

Preheat the oven to 375°F (190°C). Heat a large ovenproof frying pan over medium-high heat for 60 seconds. Add 1 tablespoon of the olive oil and heat until almost smoking. Add the beef and sear until browned on all sides. Transfer the pan to the oven and roast for 10 minutes for medium rare. Remove from the oven and cover loosely with aluminum foil.

To serve, place a black bean cake in the center of each of 4 warmed plates. Arrange 2 or 3 thin slices of beef tenderloin over each bean cake and spoon the mango salsa alongside. *Makes 4 servings*

BLACK BEAN RICE CAKES

1 cup (8 fl oz/250 ml) water

½ cup (3½ oz/105 g) Lundberg wild-blend rice, or ¼ cup (2 oz/125 g) each wild and brown rice, rinsed

2 tablespoons olive oil

½ cup (2½ oz/75 g) mixed chopped vegetables, such as carrots, celery, onion, and/or zucchini

1 cup (7 oz/220 g) cooked black beans

1 sweet potato, baked

Salt and freshly ground pepper to taste

In a medium saucepan, bring the water to a boil. Add the rice, cover, reduce heat to low, and cook for 45 minutes. Remove from heat and let sit for 10 minutes, covered.

In a small frying pan, heat 1 tablespoon of the olive oil over medium heat and sauté the vegetables for 3 to 5 minutes, or until crisp-tender.

In a food processor, combine the black beans and sweet potato. Purée until smooth. Transfer the purée to a large bowl and stir in the rice, vegetables, salt, and pepper. Divide the mixture into 4 equal portions and flatten slightly to form cakes.

In a large ovenproof frying pan, heat the remaining 1 tablespoon olive oil over medium-high heat and cook the cakes until browned, 2 or 3 minutes on each side. Transfer the pan to the oven and bake for 5 minutes.

Makes 4 servings

WARM MISSION FIG KABOBS
WITH HONEY AND BUTTERMILK SHERBET

Introduced to California by Spanish missionaries in the late 1700s, Mission figs have black-purple skins and delicious sweet red flesh. If unavailable, substitute Calimyrna or Kadota figs. The sherbet is outstanding all by itself.

HONEY AND BUTTERMILK SHERBET
¼ cup (2 fl oz/60 ml) water
¼ cup (2 oz/60 g) sugar
½ cup (6 oz/185 g) lavender or wildflower honey
2 cups (16 fl oz/500 ml) buttermilk
2 tablespoons fresh lemon juice

4 lavender stalks, about 6 inches (15 cm) long (optional)
4 Black Mission figs, halved

To make the sherbet: In a medium saucepan, bring the water and sugar to a boil, stirring until the sugar dissolves. Remove from heat and let cool. Stir in ¼ cup (3 oz/90 g) of the honey, the buttermilk, and lemon juice. Refrigerate for at least 2 hours to chill. Freeze in an ice cream maker according to the manufacturer's instructions.

To grill: If not using lavender stalks, soak four 6-inch (15-cm) wooden skewers in water for 30 minutes. Prepare an outdoor grill. Oil the grill grids. Thread 2 fig halves onto each of the 4 lavender stalks or wooden skewers. Grill, turning once, for about 3 minutes, or until tender. To bake: Preheat the oven to 425°F (220°C). Arrange the fig halves in a baking dish, cut side up, and bake for 10 minutes.

Remove the figs from the skewers, if using, and place in a shallow bowl. Serve with a scoop of sherbet drizzled with the remaining ¼ cup (3 oz/90 g) honey.

Makes 4 servings

Stonepine Estate Resort

Carmel Valley, California

Surrounded by 330 acres in the idyllic Carmel river valley, this grand country estate offers the highest level of personal comfort and attention, exceptional cuisine, resort activities, and Stonepine Equestrian, the oldest operating thoroughbred ranch west of the Mississippi. Stonepine is a member of the prestigious Relais & Chateaux Association.

Built in 1929 by Helen Crocker Russell, of the legendary San Francisco banking family, Stonepine has been owned since 1983 by Gordon and Noel Hentschel, who restored the property and opened it in 1987 as Stonepine Estate Resort. Guests stay in private houses and cottages and an elegant villa known as Chateau Noel, which is encircled by towering stonepine trees and award-winning gardens. Mrs. Russell brought Italian stonepines back from Europe and planted the seedlings around the mansion; now eighty feet in height, the majestic trees lend their name to the estate. Guests enjoy the resort's Renaissance-style swimming pool, tennis court, soccer field, archery, volleyball court, croquet lawn, and exercise room. Nearby are the spectacularly beautiful cliffs of Big Sur, the charming village of Carmel, the Monterey Bay Aquarium, and the world-class golf courses of Spanish Bay and Pebble Beach. At Stonepine Equestrian all aspects of equine sport are taught by internationally renowned instructors. Over the years, the center has been home for some of the world's finest horses, including stakes winners Majestic Prince, Countess Nashville, and Bolero Lady. Stonepine guests can take carriage rides and moonlight hayrides, and the surrounding countryside includes miles of riding and hiking trails along the Santa Lucia mountains and the Carmel River.

Each morning a gourmet breakfast is served outside on the Wisteria Terrace or in the Breakfast Room, and afternoon tea is taken in the living room. In the evening, guests assemble for a Champagne reception before dinner in the candlelit dining room, with its elegant French oak paneling and eighteenth-century fruitwood fireplace. Chef Stephane Coupel's five-course dinners are accompanied by selections from Stonepine's extensive international wine list, and the expert service is pitch-perfect. The following dinner menu was created for Menus and Music by chef Stephane Coupel.

CHATEAU CHRISTINA

Monterey County
Pinot Noir
1 9 9 7
Franzioni Vineyard

PRODUCED AND BOTTLED BY JOYCE VINEYARDS, CARMEL VALLEY, CA.
750 ML • ALCOHOL 13.9% BY VOLUME

GEORIS

quand i lait c'est   pe tot l'monde

SAUVIGNON
BLANC

Monterey
1999

Produced and Bottled by Georis Winery
Carmel Valley, California   alcohol 13% by volume

TALBOTT

1998
Chardonnay
SLEEPY HOLLOW VINEYARD

MONTEREY WHITE TABLE WINE
PRODUCED & BOTTLED BY ROBERT TALBOTT VINEYARDS
GONZALES, CA, USA

---

1 9 9 9
BARREL AGED

CHATEAU
JULIEN
MONTEREY COUNTY
Cabernet Sauvignon

ALC. 13.0% BY VOL.

GALANTE
V I N E Y A R D S

RED ROSE HILL
1998 CARMEL VALLEY
Cabernet Sauvignon
ESTATE BOTTLED
ALC. 12.5% BY VOL. • 750ML

---

1 9 9 8
BARREL AGED

CHATEAU
JULIEN
MONTEREY COUNTY
Merlot

ALC. 13.0% BY VOL.

B E R N A R D U S

1 9 9 9
Monterey County
SAUVIGNON
BLANC

PRODUCED AND BOTTLED BY BERNARDUS WINERY
CARMEL VALLEY, CALIFORNIA. ALCOHOL 13.1% BY VOLUME

GEORIS

quand i lait c'est   pe tot l'monde

ESTATE   BOTTLED
1996
CABERNET
SAUVIGNON
Carmel Valley

grown, produced and bottled by Georis Winery
Carmel Valley, California alcohol 13.0% by volume

B E R N A R D U S

1 9 9 6
MARINUS
Carmel Valley Red Wine

ESTATE GROWN AND BOTTLED

ALCOHOL 13.2% BY VOLUME

TALBOTT

1997 VINTAGE

DIAMOND ◇T◇ ESTATE

MONTEREY CHARDONNAY TABLE WINE
ESTATE GROWN, PRODUCED & BOTTLED BY
ROBERT TALBOTT, GONZALES, CA, USA

JOULLIAN

CARMEL VALLEY
CABERNET SAUVIGNON
1995

ESTATE GROWN, PRODUCED & BOTTLED BY JOULLIAN VINEYARDS LTD. © 1988
CARMEL VALLEY, CALIFORNIA • ALCOHOL 13% BY VOLUME

Dances On Your Palate
DURNEY
VINEYARDS
1992
Estate Bottled
CARMEL VALLEY
CABERNET SAUVIGNON
750 ml Product of U.S.A. Alc. 14.5% by Vol.

PRIVATE RESERVE

Menu

Foie Gras Flan with Wild Mushroom Bisque

TALBOTT CHARDONNAY SLEEPY HOLLOW, 1997

~

Petit Feuilleté with Mussels and Clams
on a Bed of Spinach

BERNARDUS SAUVIGNON BLANC, 1998

~

Roasted Rack of Lamb with
Onion Polenta Gratin and a Rosette of Vegetables

CHATEAU CHRISTINA PINOT NOIR, 1997

~

Chocolate Truffle Cake

ARTHUR HILL GILBERT

When men drink, then they are rich
and successful and win lawsuits and
are happy and help their friends.
Quickly, bring me a beaker of wine,
so that I may wet my mind and say
something clever.   —ARISTOPHANES

FOIE GRAS FLAN WITH WILD MUSHROOM BISQUE

An elegant starter for a special occasion.

8 ounces (250 g) fresh foie gras,* chopped
4 eggs
¼ cup (2 fl oz/60 ml) Sauternes or other white dessert wine
Salt and freshly ground pepper to taste
1 teaspoon Cognac or brandy
1 cup (8 fl oz/250 ml) milk

WILD MUSHROOM BISQUE

2 tablespoons unsalted butter
8 ounces (250 g) wild mushrooms such as chanterelles or morels,
   thinly sliced
3 shallots, minced
Salt and freshly ground pepper to taste
2 tablespoons port
2 cups (16 fl oz/500 ml) chicken stock (see Basics) or
   canned low-salt chicken broth
1 cup (8 fl oz/250 ml) heavy cream

☙ Preheat the oven to 350°F (180°C). Butter four 4-ounce (125-ml) ovenproof ramekins.

☙ In a blender or food processor, combine the foie gras, eggs, wine, salt, pepper, and Cognac or brandy. Process until perfectly smooth, about 3 minutes.

☙ In a small saucepan, bring the milk to a boil over low heat. Remove from heat and stir in the foie gras mixture.

☙ Place the prepared ramekins in a baking dish and pour the foie gras custard into the ramekins. Add hot water to the baking pan to come halfway up the sides of the ramekins. Bake for 40 minutes, or until a skewer plunged into the center of a flan comes out almost clean. Remove from the oven and let cool for 10 minutes.

(continued on following page)

To make the bisque: In a large frying pan, melt the butter over medium-high heat until the foam subsides. Add the mushrooms and shallots and sauté until the liquid evaporates and the mushrooms begin to brown. Add salt and pepper. Add the port and stir to scrape up any browned bits from the bottom of the pan. Add the stock or broth and boil to reduce by half. Reduce heat to medium-low, stir in the cream, and simmer for 20 minutes. Transfer to a food processor and purée.

To serve, unmold a flan in the center of each of 4 shallow soup bowls. Spoon mushroom bisque over each flan.   *Makes 4 servings*

*Fresh foie gras can be ordered from some butcher shops, or see Resources.

Petit Feuilleté with Mussels and Clams on a Bed of Spinach

An impressive dish that is easy to make.

1 sheet thawed frozen puff pastry
1 egg, beaten with 1 teaspoon water
4 tablespoons (2 oz/60 g) unsalted butter
2 shallots, thinly sliced
1½ pounds (750 g) mussels, scrubbed and debearded
1½ pounds (750 g) clams, scrubbed
1 cup (8 fl oz/250 ml) apple cider
2 cups (16 fl oz/500 ml) heavy cream
2 bunches spinach, stemmed

⚬ Line a small baking sheet with parchment paper. On a lightly floured work surface, lay out the puff pastry sheet and brush with the egg mixture. Fold the pastry in half and, using a sharp knife, cut it into 4 triangles. Place on the prepared pan. Brush the triangle tops with the egg mixture and refrigerate for 30 minutes.

⚬ Preheat the oven to 375°F (190°C). Bake the puff pastry for 25 to 30 minutes, or until puffed and golden brown.

⚬ In a large frying pan, melt 2 tablespoons of the butter over medium heat and sauté the shallots for 2 minutes, or until translucent. Add the mussels and clams. Pour in the cider, cover, and cook for 4 minutes, or until the shells open. Using a slotted spoon, transfer the mussels and clams to a plate. Discard any shellfish that have not opened. Remove the clams and mussels from their shells.

⚬ Cook the pan liquid over high heat to reduce by half. Reduce heat to medium-low, stir in the cream, and simmer for 10 minutes. Add the shellfish, reduce heat to low, and cook for about 2 minutes, or until just heated through.

⚬ Meanwhile, in a large frying pan, melt 1 tablespoon of the butter over medium heat and sauté the spinach until it wilts, about 2 minutes.

⚬ Slice each puff pastry triangle in half horizontally. Arrange a nest of spinach on each of 4 warmed plates. Top the spinach with a pastry bottom. Swirl 1 tablespoon butter into the shellfish mixture and spoon it over the pastry. Cover each with a pastry top and serve immediately. *Makes 4 servings*

2 cups (16 fl oz/500 ml) beef stock (see Basics) or canned low-salt beef broth

1 cup (8 fl oz/250 ml) chicken stock (see Basics) or canned low-salt chicken broth

1 cup (8 fl oz/250 ml) heavy cream or half-and-half

1 teaspoon salt

1 cup (5 oz/155 g) polenta

1 tablespoon olive oil, plus more for drizzling

1 large onion, minced

1 garlic clove

1 small tomato, chopped

Salt and freshly ground black pepper

½ cup (2 oz/60 g) shredded Swiss cheese

2 racks of lamb

In a medium saucepan, bring the stocks or broths, cream, and salt to a boil. Stir in the polenta, reduce heat to low, and cook for 20 minutes, stirring constantly. Remove from heat and pour into an 8-inch (20-cm) square baking dish. Refrigerate until set.

In a medium sauté pan or skillet, heat the 1 tablespoon olive oil over medium heat and sauté the onion until soft, about 5 minutes. Add the garlic and sauté for about 2 minutes. Add the tomato, salt, and pepper and cook the onion compote for 30 minutes.

Preheat the oven to 350°F (180°C). Line a baking sheet with parchment paper. Cut the polenta into sixteen 2-inch (5-cm) squares. Arrange 8 squares on the prepared pan, top each square with onion compote, and cover with a second polenta square. Sprinkle each square with cheese and bake for 25 minutes.

Meanwhile, arrange the racks of lamb in a roasting pan, sprinkle with salt and pepper, and roast until an instant-read thermometer inserted in the center of a rack and not touching bone registers 130°F (54°C) for rare, or 140°F (60°C) for medium rare. Remove from the oven and transfer to a platter. Cover loosely with aluminum foil and let rest for 5 to 10 minutes before slicing each rack into 8 chops.

To serve, arrange 4 lamb chops and 2 polenta squares on each of 4 warmed plates. Drizzle a little olive oil over the lamb, if you like, and serve immediately. *Makes 4 servings*

CHOCOLATE TRUFFLE CAKE

A splendid, rich cake.

3 eggs
½ cup (4 oz/125 g) plus 1 tablespoon sugar
6 ounces (185 g) bittersweet chocolate, chopped
4 tablespoons (2 oz/60 g) unsalted butter
¼ teaspoon salt
⅛ teaspoon cream of tartar
⅔ cup (3 oz/90 g) cake flour
1 cup (8 fl oz/250 ml) heavy cream

CHOCOLATE TRUFFLE

1 cup (8 oz/250 ml) heavy cream
12 ounces (375 g) bittersweet chocolate, chopped
1½ cups (12 fl oz/375 ml) whipped cream

❧ Preheat the oven to 350°F (180°C). Butter an 8-inch (20-cm) round cake pan and dust with flour, tapping out the excess.

❧ Separate the eggs, putting the yolks in a large bowl and the whites in another large bowl. In a small saucepan, melt the chocolate with the butter over low heat. Set aside and let cool.

❧ Beat the sugar and egg yolks together until the mixture forms a slowly dissolving ribbon on the surface when the beater is lifted. Beat in the melted chocolate and butter. In a large bowl, beat the egg whites until foamy. Add the salt and cream of tartar and beat until soft peaks form. Sprinkle in the sugar and beat until stiff, glossy peaks form.

❧ Stir one-fourth of the egg whites into the chocolate mixture. Fold in one-fourth of the flour. Fold in the remaining whites and flour until blended. Pour the batter into the prepared pan and bake for 30 minutes, or until a skewer inserted in the center comes out clean. Remove from the oven and let cool for 5 minutes. Unmold the cake onto a cake rack.

❧ To make the chocolate truffle: In a small saucepan, bring the cream to a boil over medium heat. Stir in the chocolate until smooth. Remove from heat and let cool completely. Fold in the whipped cream.

❧ Spread the chocolate mixture on the top and sides of the cake. Smooth with a spatula dipped in hot water. Refrigerate the cake for at least 1 hour before serving.   *Makes one 8-inch (20-cm) cake*

Youngberg Hill Vineyards & Inn

McMinnville, Oregon

Kevin and Tasha Byrd have created a romantic, restful inn and working vineyard in the heart of Oregon wine country. Surrounded by fifty acres of vineyards and rolling hills, the contemporary hilltop estate has panoramic views of the Willamette Valley, Mount Hood, the Coast Range, and Youngberg's stellar Pinot Noir vineyards.

Built in 1989, the sprawling shingled house has seven charming guest rooms and spacious suites, a library with massive stone fireplace, wrap-around outdoor decks, and a wine cellar that makes a wonderful setting for a private dinner. Trails wander for miles through the property and neighboring farms, and visitors spot lynx, red-tailed hawks, ring-necked pheasants, and mule deer while enjoying this peaceful retreat. Youngberg Hill is a perfect homebase for touring the many acclaimed wineries of Yamhill county. Guests also enjoy antiquing, balloon rides, golfing, cycling, exploring the beautiful Oregon coast, and visiting local art galleries and the historic district of McMinnville with its many shops and restaurants.

Each morning a full country breakfast is served in the dining room at a large central table with dreamy views of the surrounding countryside. Kevin and Tasha Byrd share the cooking of the leisurely, three-course meal which highlights fresh, local ingredients. The following breakfast menu was created by Kevin Byrd.

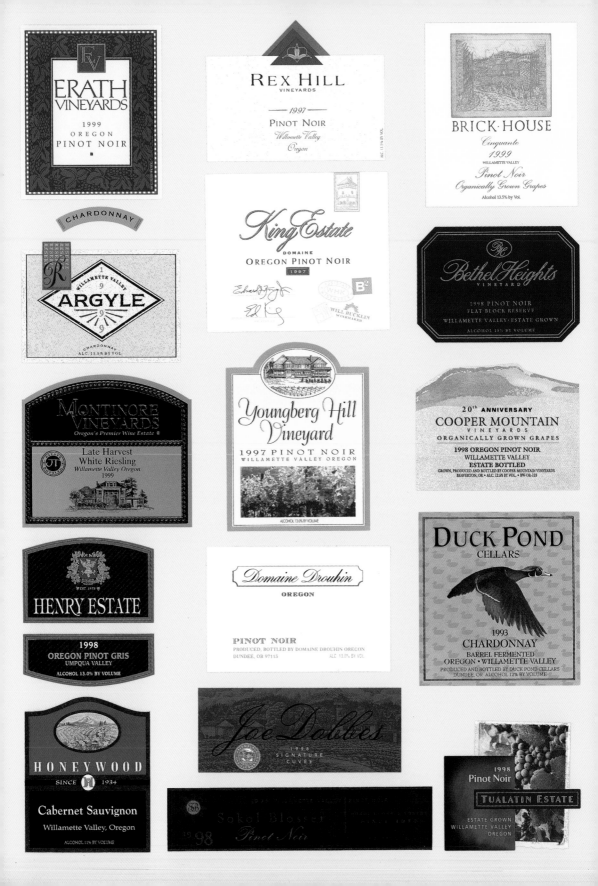

Breakfast Menu

Chocolate-Zucchini Muffins

Pears in Red Wine

Baked Caramel French Toast
with Fresh Fruit

Oscar Flores-Fiol

Eat thy bread with joy, and drink thy wine
with a merry heart. ECCLESIASTES, 9:10

# CHOCOLATE-ZUCCHINI MUFFINS

1 ¼ cups (6 ½ oz / 200 g) all-purpose flour
¼ teaspoon salt
1 ¼ teaspoons baking powder
¾ teaspoon baking soda
½ teaspoon ground cinnamon
¼ cup (¾ oz / 20 g) unsweetened cocoa powder
6 tablespoons (3 oz / 90 g) unsalted butter at room temperature
1 cup (8 oz / 250 g) sugar
1 teaspoon vanilla extract
2 eggs
¼ cup (2 fl oz / 60 ml) milk
1 cup (5 oz / 155 g) grated zucchini

❧ Preheat the oven to 350°F (180°C). Lightly butter 12 muffin cups.
❧ In a medium bowl, combine the flour, salt, baking powder, baking soda, cinnamon, and cocoa. In a large bowl, beat the butter, sugar, and vanilla together until fluffy. Beat in the eggs and stir in the milk. Stir in the flour mixture just until blended; the batter should be slightly lumpy. Gently stir in the zucchini, spoon the batter into the prepared muffin cups. Bake for 20 to 25 minutes, or until a skewer inserted in the center comes out clean.   *Makes 12 muffins*

PEARS IN RED WINE

Serve as a fruit course for breakfast, or at dinner as a lovely, light dessert.

3 cups (24 fl oz / 750 ml) dry red wine
½ cup (4 oz / 125 g) sugar
½ teaspoon grated lemon zest
4 whole cloves
1 cinnamon stick, cracked
8 black peppercorns
½ teaspoon vanilla extract
4 firm, ripe pears

❧ In a large saucepan, combine the wine, sugar, lemon zest, cloves, cinnamon, peppercorns, and vanilla. Bring to a boil and cook to reduce by half. Add the pears to the wine mixture, reduce heat to just below simmering, and cook for 20 minutes, or until pears are tender when pierced.
❧ Using a slotted spoon, transfer the pears to 4 shallow bowls. Strain the sauce through a fine-mesh sieve. Pour a little sauce over each pear and serve warm.
Makes 4 servings

BAKED CARAMEL FRENCH TOAST
WITH FRESH FRUIT

Made without too much fuss, this dish is sure to please.

1 cup (7 oz/220 g) packed brown sugar
½ cup (4 oz/125 g) unsalted butter
1 teaspoon ground cinnamon
¼ teaspoon ground nutmeg
2 tablespoons light corn syrup
2 cups (12 oz/375 g) sliced fresh fruit, such as peaches, pears, pineapple,
   and/or apples
3 eggs, lightly beaten
1 cup (8 fl oz/250 ml) milk
1 teaspoon vanilla extract
6 to 8 slices day-old French bread or whole-wheat bread
Powdered sugar for dusting

Preheat the oven to 350°F (180°C). In a small saucepan, combine the brown sugar, butter, cinnamon, nutmeg, and corn syrup. Cook over medium heat for 5 minutes, stirring occasionally. Pour into the bottom of a 9-by-13-inch (23-by-33-cm) baking dish and tilt to coat the bottom. Arrange the sliced fruit evenly on top.

In a shallow bowl, lightly beat the eggs with the milk and vanilla. Dip the bread slices into the egg mixture until thoroughly soaked on both sides. Arrange the bread in one layer over the fruit.

Bake for 30 minutes, or until lightly browned. Place 1 serving on each of 6 plates. Spoon some of the sugar syrup over each serving, dust with powdered sugar, and serve at once. *Makes 6 servings*

Basics

Artichoke Hearts

4 artichokes
1 lemon, halved

Slice the stems off the 4 artichokes. Pull off the outer leaves, then cut off the remaining cone of leaves on top. Using a teaspoon, dig out the choke. Rub the artichokes all over with the halves of 1 cut lemon to prevent discoloration. Cook the artichokes in a large pot of salted boiling water until tender when pierced, about 30 minutes. Drain well.   *Makes 4 artichoke hearts*

Brown Butter

In a large skillet, melt the butter over medium heat. Cook until browned, shaking the pan constantly so the solids do not rest on the bottom of the pan and burn.

Candied Citrus Peel

2 grapefruits, 3 oranges, or 6 lemons
2 cups (16 oz/500 g) sugar
¾ cup (6 fl oz/180 ml) water

Using a sharp knife, cut off the peel of the citrus fruit in large strips. Cook the peel in simmering water for 30 minutes. Drain, then cook in simmering water for 10 minutes. Drain and cut the peel into strips about ¼ inch wide and 2 inches long. In a saucepan, combine 1 cup (8 oz/250 g) of the sugar and the water. Bring to a simmer, add the peel, and cook until most of the sugar syrup is absorbed. Cover the pan and let stand overnight. The next day, bring the peels to a simmer. Remove from heat, let cool, and drain. Spread 1 cup (8 oz/250 g) sugar out on several thicknesses of paper towels and roll the peel in it to evenly coat all pieces. Let dry. Store in an airtight container for several months.   *Makes about 2 cups*

CINNAMON SUGAR

In a small bowl, stir ½ cup (4 oz / 125 g) sugar and 2 tablespoons ground cinnamon together until well blended.   *Makes about ⅔ cup (5 oz / 155 g)*

CITRUS ZEST

Using a zester, vegetable peeler, or sharp paring knife, cut thin strips of the colored part (the zest) of the citrus peel; don't include the white pith underneath, which is apt to be bitter.

CLARIFIED BUTTER

Clarified butter is used for cooking at high temperatures, as it will not burn. In a small, heavy saucepan, melt unsalted butter over low heat. Remove the pan from heat and let stand for several minutes. Skim off the foam and pour off the clear liquid, leaving the milky solids in the bottom of the pan. Cover and store in the refrigerator indefinitely. When clarified, butter loses about one-fourth of its original volume.

CRÈME FRAÎCHE

Lightly tangy thickened cream is used in sauces and as a topping for both savory and sweet dishes. It can be found in specialty foods stores and some grocery stores. To make crème fraîche at home, mix 2 cups (16 fl oz / 500 ml) heavy cream with 2 tablespoons buttermilk in a medium bowl. Cover with plastic wrap and let stand at room temperature overnight or until fairly thick. Refrigerate for at least 4 hours before serving. The cream can be kept in the refrigerator for several days.   *Makes 2 cups (16 oz / 500 g)*

CROSTINI

Cut 1 day-old French baguette into ¼-inch-thick (6-mm) slices. Brush lightly with olive oil. Arrange the bread on a baking sheet and bake in a preheated 375°F (190°C) oven for about 10 minutes, or until lightly golden; let cool. Store in an airtight container.   *Makes 36 to 40 toasts*

Dicing a Mango

Hold the mango upright on a cutting board with a narrow side facing you. Using a large knife, cut off one "face" (the flat side) of the fruit. Repeat on the other flat side. Score the flesh of each half into squares and push each half inside out so it looks like a hedgehog. Cut off each square.

Jerk Seasoning

1/4 cup (2 oz/60 g) packed brown sugar
2 teaspoons cayenne pepper
2 teaspoon paprika
2 teaspoons ground allspice
1 teaspoon garlic powder
1 teaspoon ground black pepper
1 teaspoon dried thyme
1 teaspoon ground ginger
1 teaspoon ground cinnamon
1 teaspoon ground nutmeg
1/2 teaspoon ground cloves

In a small bowl, combine all the ingredients. *Makes about ½ cup (¾ oz/20 g)*

Peeling and Seeding Tomatoes

Cut out the cores of the tomatoes and cut an X in the opposite end. Drop the tomatoes into a pot of rapidly boiling water for 10 seconds, or until the skin by the X peels away slightly. Drain and run cold water over the tomatoes; the skin should slip off easily. To seed, cut the tomatoes in half crosswise, hold each half upside down over the sink (or a fine-mesh sieve over a bowl, if you want to save the juice), and gently squeeze and shake to remove the seeds.

To Roast Chestnuts

Using a sharp knife, mark an X on the flat side of each chestnut, making sure to puncture the skin to reach the meat of the chestnut. Arrange the chestnuts in a single layer in a baking dish and bake in the preheated oven for 10 minutes, or until the skins peel back at the X. Remove from the oven and let cool. Peel off the skins.

To Roast Peppers and Chilies

Roast whole peppers or chilies on a grill, directly over the flame on a gas stove, or in a cast-iron skillet over medium-high heat, turning to char on all sides. Or, cut large peppers or chilies into fourths, seed, press to flatten, and char under a preheated broiler. Using tongs, transfer the peppers or chilies to a paper or plastic bag, close it, and let the peppers or chilies cool for 10 to 15 minutes. Remove from the bag, peel off the skin with your fingers or a small, sharp knife, and core and seed the peppers or chilies if charred whole.

To Section Citrus Fruit

Cut off the top and bottom of an orange, grapefruit, or lemon down to the flesh, then stand the fruit upright and cut off the peel vertically down to the flesh. Working over a bowl, hold the fruit in one hand and cut between the membranes to release the segments into the bowl. Pick out any seeds.

To Skin Peaches

Using a sharp knife, cut an X in the stem end of each peach. Drop the peaches into a pot of rapidly boiling water for about 10 seconds, or until the skin by the X peels away slightly. Transfer the peaches to a bowl of cold water; the skin should slip off easily.

Toasting Nuts and Seeds

Toasting intensifies the flavor of nuts and seeds.

Spread the nuts on a baking sheet and bake in a preheated 350°F (180°C) oven, stirring once or twice, for 5 to 10 minutes, or until fragrant and very lightly browned.

STOCKS

REDUCED STOCK OR BROTH

Use unsalted or low-salt stock or broth. Cook over medium heat at a low boil until reduced by about one-third, or until rich and well flavored.

BEEF STOCK

4 pounds (2 kg) meaty beef shanks, sliced
2 tablespoons olive oil
1 onion, chopped
1 carrot, peeled and chopped
1 celery stalk, chopped
1 bay leaf
3 fresh flat-leaf parsley sprigs
6 black peppercorns
½ cup (4 fl oz / 125 ml) dry white wine
3 quarts (3 l) water
½ cup (4 fl oz / 125 ml) tomato purée
Salt and freshly ground black pepper to taste

Preheat the oven to 400°F (200°C). In a roasting pan, toss the bones with the olive oil. Roast for 30 to 40 minutes, or until well browned, turning occasionally. Transfer to a stockpot.

Pour the fat out of the roasting pan. Place the pan over medium heat, add the wine, and stir to scrape up the browned bits from the bottom of the pan. Pour this liquid into the stockpot. Add all the remaining ingredients. Bring to a boil and skim off any foam that rises to the top. Simmer slowly for 3 to 4 hours, or until the stock is well flavored.

Strain through a sieve into a bowl and let cool. Refrigerate overnight. Remove the congealed fat on the surface. Store in the refrigerator for up to 3 days. To keep longer, bring to a boil every 3 days or freeze for up to 3 months.

Makes about 4 cups (32 fl oz / 1 l)

CHICKEN STOCK

2 onions, coarsely chopped

Bouquet garni: 4 parsley sprigs, 4 peppercorns, 1 thyme sprig, and
1 bay leaf, tied in a cheesecloth square

4 pounds (2 kg) chicken bones and bony pieces such as backs, necks,
and wings

2 carrots, peeled and chopped

3 celery stalks, chopped

5 garlic cloves

In a stockpot, combine all the ingredients and add water to cover by 2 inches
(5 cm). Bring to a boil and skim off any foam that forms on the surface.
Reduce heat to low and simmer, uncovered, for 1½ to 2 hours, or until the
stock is well flavored. Strain through a fine-mesh sieve into a clean container.
Let cool, cover, and refrigerate overnight. Remove the congealed fat from the
surface. Store in the refrigerator for up to 3 days. To keep longer, bring to a
boil every 3 days, or freeze for up to 3 months. *Makes about 2½ quarts (2.5 l)*

VEGETABLE STOCK

1 cup (5 oz/155 g) coarsely chopped carrot

1 cup (5 oz/155 g) chopped celery

2 unpeeled onions, quartered, or 2 leeks, cleaned and chopped

1 cup (5 oz/155 g) peeled and chopped parsnip

1 cup (5 oz/155 g) peeled and chopped rutabaga or turnip

2 cups (10 oz/315 g) vegetable scraps and trimmings

2 or 3 fresh parsley sprigs

1 or 2 bay leaves

½ teaspoon minced fresh thyme

½ teaspoon ground pepper

8 cups (64 fl oz/2 l) water, or more as needed

In a large stockpot, combine all the ingredients and bring to a boil. Reduce
heat to low and simmer for 1 to 2 hours. Remove from heat and strain
through a fine-mesh sieve.

Cover and refrigerate for up to 3 days. To keep longer, bring the stock to a
boil every 3 days, or freeze for up to 3 months. *Makes about 8 cups (64 fl oz/2 l)*

Conversion Charts

WEIGHT MEASUREMENTS

Standard U.S.	Ounces	Metric
1 ounce	1	30 g
¼ pound	4	125 g
½ pound	8	250 g
1 pound	16	500 g
1½ pounds	24	750 g
2 pounds	32	1 kg
2½ pounds	40	1.25 kg
3 pounds	48	1.5 kg

VOLUME MEASUREMENTS

Standard U.S.	Fluid Ounces	Metric
1 tablespoon	½	15 ml
2 tablespoons	1	30 ml
3 tablespoons	1½	45 ml
¼ cup (4 tablespoons)	2	60 ml
6 tablespoons	3	90 ml
½ cup (8 tablespoons)	4	125 ml
1 cup	8	250 ml
1 pint (2 cups)	16	500 ml
4 cups	32	1 l

OVEN TEMPERATURES

Fahrenheit	Celsius	Gas Mark
250°	120°	½
275°	135°	1
300°	150°	2
325°	165°	3
350°	180°	4
375°	190°	5
400°	200°	6
425°	220°	7

Note: For ease of use, measurements have been rounded off.

CONVERSION FACTORS

OUNCES TO GRAMS: Multiply the ounce figure by 28.3 to get the number of grams.

POUNDS TO GRAMS: Multiply the pound figure by 453.59 to get the number of grams.

POUNDS TO KILOGRAMS: Multiply the pound figure by 0.45 to get the number of kilograms.

OUNCES TO MILLILITERS: Multiply the ounce figure by 30 to get the number of milliliters.

CUPS TO LITERS: Multiply the cup figure by 0.24 to get the number of liters.

FAHRENHEIT TO CELSIUS: Subtract 32 from the Fahrenheit figure, multiply by 5, then divide by 9 to get the Celsius figure.

CONTRIBUTORS

INNS AND RESORTS

The Aerie Resort
P.O. Box 108
Malahat, British Columbia
V0R 2L0 Canada
Phone: (800) 518-1933 or (250) 743-7115
Fax: (250) 743-4766
www.aerie.bc.ca

Applewood Inn & Restaurant
13555 Highway 116
Guerneville, CA 95446
Phone: (800) 555-8509 or (707) 869-9093
Fax: (707) 869-9170
www.applewoodinn.com

Auberge du Soleil
180 Rutherford Hill Road
Rutherford, CA 94573
Phone: (800) 348-5406 or (707) 963-1211
Fax: (707) 963-8764
www.aubergedusoleil.com

Belhurst Castle
P.O. Box 609
Geneva, NY 14456
Phone: (315) 781-0201
Fax: (315) 781-0201, ext. 333
www.belhurstcastle.com

Bernardus Lodge
P.O. Box 80
Carmel Valley, CA 93924
Phone: (888) 648-9463 or (831) 658-3400
Fax: (831) 659-3529
www.bernardus.com

Birchfield Manor Country Inn
2018 Birchfield Road
Yakima, WA 98901
Phone: (800) 375-3420 or (509) 452-1960
Fax: (509) 452-2334
www.birchfieldmanor.com

Clifton, The Country Inn & Estate
1296 Clifton Inn Drive
Charlottesville, VA 22911
Phone: (888) 971-1800 or (804) 971-1800
Fax: (804) 971-7098
www.cliftoninn.com

Gaige House Inn
13540 Arnold Drive
Glen Ellen, CA 95442-9305
Phone: (800) 935-0237 or (707) 935-0237
Fax: (707) 935-6411
www.gaige.com

The Harbor House Inn
P.O. Box 369
Elk, CA 95432
Phone: (800) 720-7474 or (707) 877-3203
Fax: (707) 877-3452
www.theharborhouseinn.com

The Ink House
1575 St. Helena Highway
St. Helena, CA 94574-9775
Phone: (707) 963-3890
Fax: (707) 968-0739
www.inkhouse.com

Inn on the Twenty
3845 Main Street
Jordan, Ontario
L0R 1S0 Canada
Phone: (800) 701-8074 or (905) 562-5336
Fax: (905) 562-0009
www.innonthetwenty.com

The Kenwood Inn & Spa
10400 Sonoma Highway
Kenwood, CA 95452-9027
Phone: (800) 353-6966 or (707) 833-1293
Fax: (707) 833-1247
www.kenwoodinn.com

Madrona Manor
Wine Country Inn & Restaurant
1001 Westside Road
Healdsburg, CA 95448
Phone: (800) 258-4003 or (707) 433-4231
Fax: (707) 433-0703
www.madronamanor.com

The Maidstone Arms
Inn and Restaurant
207 Main Street
East Hampton, NY 11937
Phone: (631) 324-5006
Fax: (631) 324-5037
www.maidstonearms.com

Meadowood Napa Valley
900 Meadowood Lane
St. Helena, CA 94574
Phone: (800) 458-8080 or (707) 963-3646
Fax: (707) 963-3532
www.meadowood.com

Oak Knoll Inn
2200 East Oak Knoll Avenue
Napa Valley, CA 94558
Phone: (707) 255-2200
Fax: (707) 255-2296
www.oakknollinn.com

Rose Inn
P.O. Box 6576
Ithaca, NY 14851-6576
Phone: (607) 533-7905
Fax: (607) 533-7908
www.roseinn.com

Simpson House Inn
121 East Arrellaga Street
Santa Barbara, CA 93101
Phone: (800) 676-1280 or (805) 963-7067
Fax: (805) 564-4811
www.simpsonhouseinn.com

Sonoma Mission Inn & Spa
P.O. Box 1447
Sonoma, CA 95476-1447
Phone: (800) 862 4945 or (707) 938-9000
Fax: (707) 938-4250
www.sonomamissioninn.com

Stonepine Estate Resort
150 East Carmel Valley Road
Carmel Valley, CA 93924
Phone: (831) 659-2245
Fax: (831) 659-5160
www.stonepinecalifornia.com

Youngberg Hill Vineyards & Inn
10660 S.W. Youngberg Hill Road
McMinnville, OR 97128
Phone: (888) 657-8668 or (503) 472-2727
Fax: (503) 472-1313
www.youngberghill.com

ABOUT THE ARTISTS

Charles Beck
The Charles Beck Studio
3595 Joy Road
Occidental, CA 95465
(707) 874-1678
www.sonic.net/~chasbeck
Well known for his Sonoma County landscapes, Charles Beck works in various medias including woodcuts, acrylics, oils, and watercolors. (pages 104 and 150)

Bill Brennen
2101 West Logan
Yakima, WA 98902
(509) 453-6187
blutrop@aol.com
Bill Brennen, a Yakima Valley native, has exhibited in galleries across the United States and has work in the collections of corporations and individuals. (page 91)

Kay Carlson
331 Industrial Center Building
480 Gate 5 Road
Sausalito, CA 94965
(415) 331-9520
kaycarlson@kaycarlson.com
Educated at the San Francisco Art Institute, Kay Carlson is a California colorist whose landscapes are in many private, corporate, and university collections. (pages 140 and 210)

Stephen Dominick
Stephen Dominick Studio
Niagara-on-the-Lake, Canada
(905) 468-8487
www.stephendominick.com
Stephen Dominick is a renowned Canadian portrait photographer based in Niagara-on-the-Lake. He has photographed many celebrities and is currently working on several book projects. (page 134)

Oscar Flores-Fiol
Appleridge Studio
36250 S.E. Douglass Road
Eagle Creek, OR 97022-9604
(503) 637-3373
www.flores-fiol.com
Oscar Flores-Fiol was raised in Peru and received a fine arts degree from Portland State University, Oregon. Mr. Flores-Fiol's paintings can be found in the collections of individuals and corporations throughout the world. (page 230)

Alex Fong
2465 Quail Place
Kelowna, British Columbia
V1V 1Z7 Canada
(250) 491-0866
fongsworld@home.com
Alex Fong's translucent, impressionistic paintings have colored flecks, which he calls "confetti," to represent his celebration of life. Fong was a touring member of the Western Lights Artist's Group, and is involved with music, theater, food, wine, and art education in the Okanagan Valley. (page 71)

Arthur Hill Gilbert
(1894–1970) After a career as a Naval officer, Arthur Hill Gilbert was educated at the Otis Art Institute in California and the Chicago Art Institute. A National Academician, Gilbert was a founding member of the Carmel Art Association. He is well known for his landscape paintings of California's golden hills and live oak trees. (page 220)

Steven Gordon
The Gordon Gallery
6484 Washington Street, Suite C
Yountville, CA 94599
(707) 944-0823
tggallery@aol.com
Steven Gordon has a Bachelor of Arts in art from the University of Wisconsin and a Master of Fine Arts from Washington University in St. Louis. His pastel landscapes are exhibited across the country, as well as at his own gallery in the Napa Valley. (pages 122 and 178)

Brian Lamprell
P.O. Box 60925
Palo Alto, CA 94306
(650) 473-1072
Brian Lamprell was born in England and studied at the Birmingham School of Architecture. He practices as an architect and illustrator in Palo Alto, California and has exhibited extensively in the United States and in England. (page 114)

Michael Masicampo
1326 Oceanaire
San Luis Obispo, CA 93405
(805) 565-1580
Michael Masicampo has been an artist-in-residence for the Edna Valley Arroyo Grande Valley Vinters' Association, and his work is shown and collected in the San Luis Obispo region. (page 26)

Anne Miller
126 4100 24 Avenue
Vernon, British Columbia
Canada V1T 8J6
amillerwatercolours@hotmail.com
For twelve years, Canadian native Anne Miller painted watercolors in her studio aboard a sailboat in the Caribbean. She has since returned to British Columbia, where she paints the landscapes of the Okanagan Valley. (page 36)

Frederick Nichols
Frederick Nichols Studio
P.O. Box 78
5420 Governor Barbour Street
Barboursville, VA 22923
(540) 832-3565 or (888) 994-3733
www.frednichols.com
Frederick Nichols, a graduate of the Pratt Institute and the Ecoles des Beaux Arts in Fontainebleau, France, has works in the collections of the Mississippi Museum of Art and the Tama Art University Museum in Tokyo, among others. Nichols maintains a studio, print-making workshop, and gallery in Barboursville, Virginia. (page 96)

Carol Parker
110 Calera Canyon Road
Salinas, CA 93908
(831) 484-9761
cparker110@aol.com
Carol Parker is a watercolorist working in the Monterey Peninsula area. She studied art at California State University at Chico and graduated with a Bachelor of Arts from San Jose State University. Parker paints landscapes, still life, and figurative works. (page 76)

Ralph Pugliese, Jr.
East End Greetings
P.O. Box 481
Cutchogue, NY 11935
www.ralphjr.com
A well-known Long Island photographer, Ralph Pugliese, Jr. specializes in landscapes, as well as architectural, and industrial imagery. (page 160)

Kristian S. Reynolds
Reynolds Media
2035 Woodchuck Hill Road
Cortland, NY 13045
(607) 849-3759
Kristian S. Reynolds has a Bachelor of Arts in professional photography from the Rochester Institute of Technology. He lives in New York's Finger Lakes region and specializes in landscapes, sports, recreation, and industrial imagery. Reynolds's book, *Finger Lakes Panoramas*, captures the exceptional beauty of the region. (page 190)

Justina Selinger
Justina Selinger Studios
P.O. Box 723
Occidental, CA 95465
(707) 874-3718
Educated at the School of Light and Color in California and the Cape Cod School of Art in Provincetown, Justina Selinger is an award-winning artist whose primary focus is the effect of light on color. (page 51)

Earl Thollander
A well-known book illustrator, Earl Thollander has lived and painted in the Napa Valley for over thirty years. (pages 61 and 170)

Sue Treuhaft
507 South Lucas
Santa Maria, CA 93454
(805) 928-8683
A muralist who works with businesses and home-owners, Sue Treuhaft also paints landscapes in California's central coast region. (page 205)

Resources

Regional Wine Associations

British Columbia
British Columbia Wine Institute
601 West Broadway, Suite 400
Vancouver, British Columbia
V5Z 4C2 Canada
Phone: (800) 811-9911 or (604) 664-7744
Fax: (604) 903-7396

California
Anderson Valley Winegrowers Association
P.O. Box 63
Philo, CA 95466-0063
Phone: (707) 895-9463
Fax: (707) 895-9463
www.avwines.com

Monterey County Vintners and Growers
Association
P.O. Box 1793
Monterey, California 93942
Phone: (831) 375-9400
Fax: (831) 375-1116
www.montereywines.org

The Napa Valley Conference & Visitors
Bureau
1310 Napa Town Center
Napa, CA 94559
Tel: (707) 226-7459
www.napavalley.com

Russian River Wine Road
P.O. Box 46
Healdsburg, CA 95448
Phone: (800) 723-6336 or (707) 433-4335
www.wineroad.com

Santa Barbara County Vintners Association
P.O. Box 1558
Santa Ynez, CA 93460-1558
Phone: (800) 218-0881 or (805) 688-0881
Fax (805) 686-5881
www.sbcountywines.com

Sonoma County Wineries Association
5000 Roberts Lake Road
Rohnert Park, CA 94928
Phone: (800) 939-7666 or (707) 586-3795
Fax: (707) 586-1383
www.sonomawine.com

New York
New York Wine & Grape Foundation
350 Elm Street
Penn Yan, NY 14527
Phone: (315) 536-7442
Fax: (315) 536-0719
www.newyorkwines.org

Cayuga Wine Trail
P.O. Box 123
Fayette, NY 13065
Phone: (800) 684-5217
www.cayugawine.com

Keuka Lake Wine Trail
2375 Route 14A
Penn Yan, NY 14527
Phone: (800) 440-4898
www.keukawinetrail.com

Long Island Wine Council
P.O. Box 74
Peconic, NY 11958
Phone: (631) 369-5887
www.liwines.com

Seneca Lake Winery Association
Keuka Business Park, Suite 100
Penn Yan, NY 14527
Phone: (877) 536-2717 or (315) 536-9996
www.senecalakewine.com

Ontario
Wine Council of Ontario
110 Hannover Drive, Suite B205
St. Catharines, Ontario
L2W 1A4 Canada
Phone: (905) 684-8070
Fax: (905) 684-2993
www.wineroute.com

Oregon
Oregon Wine Advisory Board
1200 N.W. Naito Parkway, Suite 400
Portland, OR 97209
Phone: (800) 242-2363 or (503) 228-8336
Fax: (503) 228-8337
www.oregonwine.org

Yamhill County Wineries Association
P.O. Box 25162
Portland, OR 97298
Phone: (503) 646-2985
Fax: (503) 292-0713
www.yamhillwine.com

Virginia
Virginia Wine Marketing Office
P.O. Box 1163
Richmond, VA 23218
Phone: (800) 828-4637 or (804) 786-7380
www.virginiawines.org

Washington
Washington Wine Commission
500 Union Street, Suite 945
Seattle, WA 98101
Phone: (206) 667-9463
Fax: (206) 583-0573
www.washingtonwine.org

Columbia Valley Winery Association
P.O. Box 6644
Kennewick, WA 99336
Phone: (866) 360-6611 or (509) 585-0903
Fax: (509) 585-8744
www.columbiavalleywine.com

Yakima Valley Winery Association
P.O. Box 39
Grandview, WA 98930
Phone: (800) 258-7270
www.yakimavalleywine.com

Online

www.wineanswers.com
Information about varieties, regions, food
affinities, and other aspects of wine is provided
by the Wine Market Council, a nonprofit orga-
nization representing the U.S. wine trade.

www.winejournal.com
Dorothy J. Gaiter and John Brecher, who write
the weekly "Tastings" column for *The Wall Street
Journal,* provide practical advice on choosing
wines for dining and entertaining.

www.winespectator.com
The online version of *Wine Spectator* magazine.

Resources for Cooks

Cherry Republic
P.O. Box 677
Glen Arbor, MI 49636-0677
(800) 206-6949 or (231) 334-3150
www.cherryrepublic.com
Dried cherries, salsas, salad dressings, cherry
jams, and chocolate-covered cherries.

D'Artagnan
280 Wilson Avenue
Newark, NJ 07105
Phone: (800) 327-8246 or (973) 344-0565
www.dartagnan.com
Foreign and domestic foie gras, confit of
goose or duck, fresh duck, dried and fresh
(in season) mushrooms; overnight delivery.

Penzey's Spices
(800) 741-7787
www.penzeys.com
Dried herbs and spices, including epazote,
jerk seasoning, and brown mustard seeds.
Spice blends and seasonings.

The Wine Enthusiast
P.O. Box 39
Pleasantville, NY 10570
Phone: (800) 356-8466 or (914) 345-9463
www.wineenthusiast.com
Stemware, wine racks, home wine cellars,
and other wine accessories.

ACKNOWLEDGMENTS

I would like to thank the many people who made this volume possible. My deepest gratitude to the proprietors, chefs, wine directors, and sommeliers of the restaurants who generously contributed their recipes and wine suggestions to the cookbook: Markus Griesser, Christophe Letard, and James Kendal; Jim Caron, Darryl Notter, and Brian Gerritsen; George A. Goeggel, John Egelhoff, and Richard Reddington; Bernardus Pon and Cal Stemenov; Duane Reeder and Casey Belile; Wil and Sandy Massett, Brad Massett, and Tim Newbury; Michael Habony, Christopher Carey, Alex Kirkland, and Donna Wagner; Ken Burnet, Greg Nemrow, and Charles Holmes; Samuel and Elle Haynes and Paul Ciardiello; Diane DeFilipi; Helen Young, Len Pennachetti, Rob Fracchioni, Anna Olson, and Michael Olson; Terry and Roseann Grimm; Coke Anne Wilcox, Bill Valentine, and Meredith Hasemann; Bill and Trudi Konrad and Jesse Malgren; Bill Harlan, Seamus McManus, Stephen Tevere, and Anne Marie Conover; Barbara and John Passino; Charles and Sherry Rosemann; Glyn and Linda Sue Davies, Linda Crocker, and Dixie Adair Budke; Ulrich Krauer and Toni Robertson; Gordon Hentschel, Daniel Barduzzi, Stephane Coupel, and Wendy Mikuls; Kevin and Tasha Byrd.

I am forever grateful to Mike Marshall for making this recording a dream come true. Affectionate thanks to Darol Anger, Paul McCandless, Phil Aaberg, and Todd Phillips. Thanks also to recording and mixing engineer David Luke, assistant engineer Dave Welhausen, and George Horn of Fantasy Studios, Berkeley, for the mastering.

Thank you Gene Burns for the foreword, for your quick wit, and for your support. Sincere thanks to Paul Moore for his stunning photographs, Amy Nathan for her extraordinary food styling, and Sara Slavin for use of her stylish tableware.

Thank you to Bob Sessions of Hanzell Vineyards, Joe Mardesich, Tim Ware, the Allied Arts Council of Yakima Valley, the Carmel Art Association, Marti Mecinski of Standing Stone Vineyards, master sommelier Peter Granoff, Women with Wine Sense, Scott Ferguson of the Napa Valley Vintner's Association, Brendan Eliason of the Winebrats, photographer Kate Kline May, David Mikan of Wines by Morrell, Easthampton, Penelope Brault, Anne and Greg Evans, Fritz Hatton, Bill and Dawnine Dyer, and Suze Kramer.

Deepest gratitude to my longtime editor Carolyn Miller for her expert advice, editorial guidance, and attention to detail. Thanks to Jenny Barry of Jennifer Barry Design for her book and cover design and for her enthusiastic support of this project. Thanks also to Kristen Wurz of Jennifer Barry Design.

I want to especially thank Sarah Creider for her many contributions and for her generous good advice during this entire project. Grateful acknowledgments to Sharlene Swacke, Connie Woods, Ned Waring, Tim Forney, Erick Villatoro, and Pia Loavenbruck of Menus and Music.

And as always, to my daughters, Claire and Caitlin, and my husband, John, for their adventurous appetites and their love.

Index